The In-Demand Coach

How to Consistently Attract Clients
and Build a 6-Figure Coaching Brand

Jason Meland

Fitness Publishing

The In-Demand Coach: How to Consistently Attract Clients and Build a 6-Figure Coaching Brand

Published by Fitness Marketing Group, Lake Ozark, MO

Printed in the United States of America

ISBN: 9798340924773

This publication is designed to provide accurate and authoritative information with regard to the subject matter covered. It is sold with the understanding that the publisher is not engaged in rendering legal, accounting, or other professional advice. If legal advice or other expert assistance is required, the services of a competent professional should be sought. This book is for informational purposes only. It is not intended to substitute the practices of your doctor, dietitian, or other health care provider. It is up to you to do your due diligence to collaborate with your personal health care providers.

First edition

For more information, contact:

In Demand Coach

Email: jason@InDemandCoach.com

Website: www.InDemandCoach.com

Table of Contents

About the Author

Preface

"Success usually comes to those who are too busy to be looking for it." — Henry David Thoreau

Running a coaching business can be **insanely challenging**, but let me tell you—when you nail it, it's **beyond worth it**.

I've been in this game for over 12 years now, and I've seen it all. I've faced the highs, the lows, and everything in between. So, I decided to take all that experience and boil it down into this book. If you're tired of the rollercoaster of *"feast or famine"* months, this is your guide to finally building a coaching business that hits consistent six-figure years (or even more, if that's what you're aiming for).

Here's the thing—I know what you're going through. I've talked to countless coaches who are in the same boat.

Maybe you're dealing with flaky clients, struggling to stand out in a sea of other coaches on social media, or worried about how to scale your business without burning out. It's a lot. But this book? It's your **no-BS** roadmap to fix all that.

We're going to cover how to attract more clients, master your messaging, and streamline your offerings so you can make more money **without losing your mind**.

Let me tell you about Emily from Chicago. She's a pro—knows her stuff and is super passionate about helping women lose weight. But her income? All over the place. She was **this close** to calling it quits.

And then there was Mike from London. He came out of the gate strong but got **swamped** with all the business stuff he wasn't prepared for. Marketing, systems, scaling—it was overwhelming.

Their stories? They're probably a lot like yours. And that's exactly why I wrote this book. It's for you, for Emily, for Mike, and for every coach who's lying in bed at night thinking, *"There's gotta be a better way."*

I've packed this book with my hard-earned lessons and the absolute **gold** I've picked up from experts in marketing, sales psychology, and business management. Massive gratitude to all of them for sharing their insights and paving the way.

To you—thanks for giving me a shot. I'm here to help you **level up** your business. Wherever you are in the world, the principles I'm laying out are designed to tackle the exact challenges you're facing and the goals you're striving for.

This book is for the coaches who already have their feet wet and are ready to make some serious waves. You know who you are and who you serve—but you're hungry to take things to the next level.

So, as you read, keep an open mind. Commit to applying these lessons, because if you do, by the end of this book, you won't just know how to **stand out**; you'll understand what makes a coaching business thrive and how to **implement** these strategies to see real, tangible results in your revenue and client satisfaction.

Let's **freaking do this**. Welcome to the next chapter of your coaching career, my friend.

Chapter One

Becoming The In-Demand Coach

Can Stability and Authority Truly Reshape a Career?

Damn, I remember those early days like they were yesterday.

Picture this: It's 5 AM, and I'm standing in my gym, staring at the rusty equipment I'd pieced together. The place reeked of sweat and determination – and maybe a little desperation, if I'm being honest.

I'd just quit my cushy firefighter career to chase this crazy dream of being a full-time fitness coach. Talk about a rollercoaster ride. One month I'd be flush with cash, the next I'd be scraping by, wondering if I'd made the biggest mistake of my life.

Those nights were the worst. Lying in bed, mind racing, wondering if my passion for helping people get fit could actually pay the bills. It was friggin' terrifying.

But here's the thing – I kept pushing. I knew deep down that if I could just figure out this business stuff, I could make a real impact. And slowly but surely, things started to click.

Fast forward a bit, and I'm approaching that magical $20K a month mark. It felt like I was finally stepping into my own as not just a coach, but a legit business owner.

Every decision I made felt bigger now. It wasn't just about training clients anymore – it was about building something sustainable, something that could really change lives on a bigger scale.

I started thinking differently too. It wasn't just about the money (though let's be real, that stability felt pretty dang good). It was about becoming a voice in the industry, someone people turned to for real advice.

As I watched my clients transform their bodies and their lives, I realized I was transforming too. From a guy with a passion and an outdoor gym to someone who was actually making waves in the fitness world.

Looking back, crossing that financial threshold wasn't just about the numbers. It was about proving to myself that I could do this – really do this. It was about turning all those doubts into confidence and showing everyone (including myself) that I wasn't just playing at being a business owner. I was one.

So yeah, money matters. But what really counts? It's the impact you make and the lives you change – including your own.

From Striving to Thriving: How Top Coaches Break the $20K Barrier

Let's cut straight to it: in the wild world of online coaching, hitting that $20K-$30K per month isn't just some number—it's the moment everything changes.

We're not talking scraping by anymore. We're talking *thriving*.

When you consistently pull in $20K+ every month, you've entered a new league. You're not worrying about how to cover bills. You're not wondering if your dream was a mistake. You're stepping into the role of an authority, a leader in your niche.

And the cash? Oh yeah, that's nice too. But the real shift is in your mind.

The Mental Shift of $20K Months

Let's get real for a sec: the biggest change isn't in your wallet—it's in your head.

Before hitting this level, you're probably on that brutal rollercoaster—one month, you're riding high, the next, you're sweating bullets about where the next client is coming from. That stress isn't just draining your energy, it's *killing* your creativity.

But when you crack that $20K+ threshold? It's like you unlock a whole new level. You're not just surviving anymore—you're thriving. You can finally focus on what actually matters instead of scrambling to keep the lights on.

Hitting this income level isn't just about money (though, let's be honest, that part *feels* good). It's about mental freedom. It's the confidence that lets you make bigger moves, take bigger risks, and build something that lasts. You can finally stop *worrying* about the bills and start *building* the future.

Building Market Authority

Here's the cold, hard truth: when you're making $20K or more every month, you're not just another coach on Instagram anymore. You're someone people *seek out*. You're a *go-to* authority.

And guess what? The clients you start attracting aren't the tire-kickers. They're serious. They're ready to invest in themselves. You've gone from just another coach in the sea of sameness to being the coach who commands attention.

Laying Down Your Success Foundations

Alright, let's get to the good stuff.

If you're grinding your way to $5K or $10K months but still feeling like you're one bad week away from disaster, trust me—I've been there. It's brutal.

But what if I told you that consistent $20K-$30K+ months are not only possible, but *inevitable* with the right system? Yeah, it sounds like hype, but I'm telling you—it's not.

Before you can build a thriving online coaching business, you need to lay down solid foundations. This is where most coaches fall short—they dive into marketing, sales, and growth tactics without having a clear strategy in place. But if you want to create consistent, scalable results, you need to start with the essentials.

There are three foundational pillars that will set you apart and allow you to attract, engage, and convert clients like clockwork:

1. **Magic Messaging**

   Your messaging is the key to everything. It's what cuts through the noise and speaks directly to your ideal clients. Magic Messaging is about more than just catchy taglines—it's about crafting a message that resonates deeply with your audience's struggles and desires. It positions you as the *only* solution to their problem. When you nail your messaging, you stop chasing clients—they start chasing you.

2. **Strategic Content Ecosystem**

   Content is the bridge between you and your audience, but not just any content—*strategic* content. This is where your messaging comes to life. Your Strategic Content Ecosystem is designed to attract the right people by providing value that educates, entertains, and builds trust. It's about having a consistent content cadence that works across platforms to create a magnetic presence that draws clients in, instead of overwhelming them with random posts.

3. **Value-First Conversion System**

   Finally, you need a system that turns interest into action. Your Value-First Conversion System is a process designed to nurture leads through authentic engagement and high-value offers, turning them into paying clients. It's about delivering results *before* they ever invest in you, proving that your methods work and building trust at every step. This system allows you to convert leads without the pressure-heavy sales tactics that feel forced or insincere.

When you lay these three pillars—Magic Messaging, a Strategic Content Ecosystem, and a Value-First Conversion System—you create a rock-solid foundation that ensures consistent lead flow, effortless conversions, and long-term business growth.

Client Attraction Marketing System

Magic Messaging Makeover

This chapter is about laying the foundation for insane growth. In the upcoming chapters, we will be diving into client acquisition that actually works, messaging that doesn't just blend in, and systems that scale *without* burning you out.

But before we do... you and I have to build the foundation. Together.

We're about to dive into what separates the struggling coaches from the ones who *thrive*.

Start With The Why (Simon Says)

First things first: your *why*.

Why are you doing this? And I'm not talking surface-level "I want to make more money" BS. That's not going to keep you going when things get tough.

What's driving you deep down? What impact do you want to make? What legacy are you trying to build?

That's the rocket fuel for your coaching business. When you know your "why," everything shifts. Your content hits harder, your sales feel natural, and your clients stick around longer because they feel that passion radiating from you.

And here's a pro tip: Get specific about why you want to hit your financial goals too. $30K months sound good, but *why* do you want that number? What does it get you? The house, the freedom, the ability to take your family on vacations, or maybe just the peace of knowing you're *secure*.

Figure that out, and you'll be unstoppable.

The Power of Your "Why"

Let's unpack "why" for a second, because it's not just some fluffy concept - when your WHY lights you up... you become unstoppable.

Think about it. Why the heck are you doing this? And again, let's go beyond the surface-level stuff like *"I want to make more money"* or *"I wanna be Instagram famous."* That crap won't keep you going when the going gets tough.

Nope, I'm talking about the real, deep-down reason that gets you fired up even on days when you feel like throwing in the towel.

Your "why" is like the engine in a high-end sports car. Without it, you're just a shiny hunk of metal sitting in the driveway. But with a powerful engine? You're ready to leave everyone else in the dust.

Let me break it down for you:

A weak "why" = Struggling to book calls, constantly chasing clients, feeling burned out

A strong "why" = Clients sliding into your DMs, consistently crushing your income goals, feeling on fire every damn day

Here's a real talk moment: When I first started, I thought I was in it for the money and the recognition. But that got old real quick. It wasn't until I tapped into my real passion - helping people transform their lives through fitness - that things really took off.

And let me tell you, when you're crystal clear on your "why," everything changes. Your content hits different. Your sales calls feel more authentic. Your clients stick around longer.

So here's your homework: Dig deep and find that fire in your belly. What gets you pumped to wake up and coach every day? What impact do you want to make in this world?

Once you're clear on that internal why... let's go a step forward.

WHY do you want to hit your "money goal." For example, if your goal is to get to $30k per month... WHY that number?

Most coaches get sucked into following what they see other people posting on the internet. 10k months. 20k months. 50k months. 100k months.

But it's incredibly hard to hit your income goal if there is NO actual motivation to hitting it.

My advice to you. Get clear on the EXACT amount of money you want to live your dream lifestyle.

What type of house do you want to live in? What type of car do you want to drive? How often do you want to travel? How much do you want to donate each month? Etc.

The more specific you can be... the more motivating your income goal will be.

Figure that out, and I promise you'll be unstoppable.

The Three M's of Being In-Demand

So, what makes a coach truly in-demand? Is it some secret formula? Expertise? Charisma? Marketing genius?

The trap that so many coaches and entrepreneurs fall into is relying way too much on strategies & tactics... and not building a solid foundation based on principles.

I'm about to walk you through the proven process that I've personally used in three different businesses, three different niches, to become in-demand. This is the exact same system that's helped hundreds of my students carve out their own sub-niches and crush it.

There are three M's that you absolutely need to master if you want to build a successful coaching business. These aren't just some fluffy concepts - they're the fundamental building blocks that'll take your business to the next level.

Mindset: Managing Your Thinking and Emotional State

Message: Communicating Your Unique Value

Money-Making Moves: The Skills That Actually Generate Income

Each of these elements is critical, and they work in synergy to create a coaching business that doesn't just survive—it thrives. Let's break them down one by one.

Mindset: The Foundation of Your Success

Here's the truth: Everything that has ever been created started as a thought. The device you're reading this on? (if on Kindle lol) It began as an idea in someone's mind. Your coaching business? It started when you first thought, *"Hey, I could do this."*

But here's where most people go wrong: They don't realize that their thinking directly impacts their results. It's a simple but powerful paradigm:

Thinking → Emotional State → Actions → Results

Your mindset isn't just about positive thinking—it's about managing your emotional state to take powerful, consistent action. When you master this, you show up differently. You communicate differently. You attract clients differently.

Action Step: Take a sticky note and write, *"What would an in-demand coach do?"* Place it where you'll see it every day. This simple reminder will start shifting your mindset and actions.

Message: Your Verbal Superpower

You need to commit right now to mastering your ability to communicate your message. This isn't just about crafting pretty Instagram posts or writing long-form content (although those can be part of it). It's about saying the right words, to the right people, in the right way.

Your message should do three things:

1. Connect with your audience on an emotional level

2. Captivate their attention in a world full of distractions

3. Convert them from passive observers to raving fans and paying clients

When you nail your messaging, you stand out in a sea of sameness. You become the go-to expert in your niche, the person people think of when they need help in your area of expertise.

Money-Making Moves: Skills That Pay the Bills

Listen up, because this is where the rubber meets the road. All the mindset work and messaging in the world won't matter if you can't turn it into cold, hard cash. That's where Money-Making Moves come in.

These are the specific skills you need to develop to generate income consistently:

- **Marketing**: Creating conversion-focused content and marketing campaigns

- **Copywriting**: Using words to turn strangers into buyers (includes speaking too)

- **Nurturing leads**: Building relationships with prospects

- **High-ticket sales**: How to sell expensive stuff to strangers.

- **Coaching**: Delivering transformational coaching experiences

- **Leadership/delegation**: Creating simple SOPs

and leading other humans

You've got to commit to consciously improving these skills every single day. Track your KPIs (Key Performance Indicators) religiously. Always be asking yourself, "How can I get better at this?"

Putting It All Together

Now, here's the thing: These Three M's don't work in isolation. They work **together** to create a business that thrives.

A strong mindset allows you to craft more compelling messages and execute your money-making moves with confidence. A powerful message attracts more opportunities to practice your money-making moves and reinforces your mindset. And when your money-making moves start paying off, it validates your mindset and proves the effectiveness of your message.

Remember, becoming an in-demand coach isn't a destination—it's a journey. There will be ups and downs. But when you focus on mastering these Three M's, you create a resilient, thriving coaching business that can weather any storm.

Your journey to becoming in-demand starts now. In the following chapters, we'll dive deeper into each of these M's, giving you practical strategies and tactics to implement in your business immediately.

Traits of an In-Demand Coach

Being in-demand isn't about having the fanciest certifications or the most knowledge (though that can help). It's about being a freaking lighthouse in a sea of mediocre coaches.

Here's what sets the multi 6 and 7-figure coaches apart:

1. They're knowledge junkies: Always learning, always growing. Not just about their craft, but about how to actually talk to people and get inside their heads.

2. They've got integrity for days: No sketchy tactics or false promises. They build trust like it's their job (because it is).

3. They're communication ninjas: They don't just talk AT audience, they get on their level and speak their language.

4. They're business savvy: They know their worth and aren't afraid to charge it. Plus, they've got their marketing game on lock.

5. They're systems-focused: They aren't chasing tactics... they're focused on building systems that create predictable results in each area of their business (lead gen, lead nurture, conversion, delivery and retention)

Now, here's the thing: These aren't just skills you're born with. You develop this over time if you're willing to put in the work.

So ask yourself: Are you ready to level up and become that lighthouse? Or are you cool with being just another buoy bobbing in the ocean?

If you're ready to make the leap, keep reading. Because I'm about to show you exactly how to transform yourself into an in-demand, six-figure coach.

Setting the Foundation for Consistent Growth (Soul-Brain-Skills Blueprint)

In the rollercoaster world of entrepreneurship, one thing remains constant: change. After 12 years in the trenches of running businesses, I've seen more ups and downs than a theme park. But here's the thing - it's not the highs that define your success, it's how you handle the lows.

Let's face it: most businesses don't make it past their first birthday. Of those that do, a significant chunk fail within three years, and even fewer make it to the five-year mark. It's a sobering reality, but it doesn't have to be your reality.

So, what's the secret sauce? How do you not just survive but thrive in this entrepreneurial jungle? Enter the Soul-Brain-Skills-Blueprint

Picture a pyramid (see image). At the top, you've got the "How" — the strategies and tactics everyone obsesses over. Below that, you've got the **Skills** — the habits and capabilities that make or break your business. Then comes the **Brain** — your psychology and beliefs that drive every move. And at the base, the foundation holding it all together, you've got the **Soul** — your nervous system and physiology.

Most people? They only focus on the top of the pyramid. The latest marketing funnel. The hottest new trend. The next shiny tactic. But here's the deal: without a solid foundation, you're building a house on sand.

Soul-Brain-Skills Blueprint

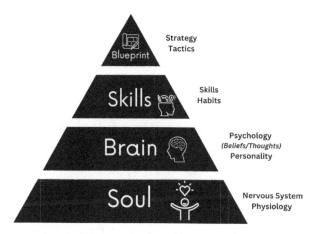

Let's break it down:

Blueprint (The HOW: Strategies and Tactics)

This is where most people live. They're constantly chasing the latest marketing funnel, the hottest social media platform, or the trendiest diet plan (if you're in the fitness space). But here's the truth: tactics without a solid foundation are like building a house on sand.

Skills (Skills and Habits)

This is where the rubber meets the road. It's about developing high-performance habits and mastering the skills that actually move the needle in your business. We're talking marketing, sales, coaching, time management - the works.

Brain (Psychology and Beliefs)

As the legendary Tony Robbins says, "Success is 80% psychology, 20% strategy." Your beliefs about money, success, and your own capabilities will shape your actions more than any tactic ever could.

Soul (Nervous System and Physiology)

This is the game-changer most entrepreneurs ignore. Your physical and emotional state is the foundation that supports everything else. Neglect this, and you're building your business on quicksand.

The Heart of the Matter

Let me get real with you for a second. There was a time in my business when things got so bad, I couldn't even pay myself. We were $45,000 in debt, and my stress levels were through the roof. But here's the craziest thing - even when things turned around financially, I still felt stressed and anxious.

Why? Because I was neglecting the base of the pyramid - my Soul.

The Million-Dollar Question

Now, I want you to ask yourself this crucial question: What is the core emotion fueling your work?

This isn't just some fluffy self-help exercise. This is about understanding the emotional engine driving your business. Are you fueled by fear and scarcity? Or by courage and abundance?

Your answer to this question will shape every aspect of your business, from how you create content to how you interact with clients.

The Entrepreneur's Consciousness

Let me illustrate this with a tale of two entrepreneurs: John and Sarah.

John operates from a survival paradigm. His content is inauthentic and inconsistent. His DMs are driven by scarcity. He over promises and under delivered to clients. He's a taker in relationships, always looking out for number one.

Sarah, on the other hand, operates from a place of reason and integrity. Her content is vulnerable, authentic, and consistent. She's generous with her audience, polarizing when necessary, but always from a place of truth. She overdelivers to clients, maintains clear boundaries, and challenges people to be their best. In relationships, she's reciprocal, giving, and trusting.

The question is: Which entrepreneur do you want to be?

Bringing It All Together

Now, it's time to put this knowledge into action. Here's what I want you to do:

1. **Implement one daily practice for Soul-level work** (meditation, breathwork, etc.)

2. **Challenge your limiting beliefs** and replace them with empowering ones.

3. **Identify the key skills** you need to develop and create a plan to improve one this month

4. **Align your strategies and tactics** with this new foundation.

5. **Answer the million-dollar question**: What's

driving your work—fear or abundance?

6. **Decide:** Do you want to be a John or a Sarah? List three actions to shift towards Sarah's approach

7. **Create a 30-day plan** to implement changes at each level of the pyramid

Remember, this isn't about perfection. It's about progress. Take it one step at a time, and you'll be amazed at how quickly things can change.

The Path to Becoming a 6-Figure Coach

Let's be real: hitting that $20K per month mark isn't just a number—it's the moment your entire business shifts. It's when you stop worrying about survival and start building something that truly lasts. More than just filling your bank account, this shift transforms your stability, confidence, and authority in the market.

But here's the key: this isn't about surface-level tactics. It's about laying down the right foundation. The "why" behind your business isn't some fluffy, motivational buzzword—it's the fuel that keeps you pushing forward when everything gets hard. A clear, powerful "why" isn't just for you; it connects you with your clients on a deeper level. You stop being just another coach, and you become *the coach* they turn to for transformation.

To hit that 6-figure consistency, it's about more than just knowing what to do—it's about becoming the kind of coach who shows up, day in and day out, ready to lead. The ones who hit this level are relentless learners, they operate with integrity, and they know how to communicate like a pro. Those aren't just skills—they're a mindset. And that mindset is what drives your success.

Building this foundation means more than chasing the latest trends. It's about mastering the Soul-Brain-Skills-Blueprint. Without that foundation, even the best tactics will fall flat. You need to take care of your mindset, master the skills that actually generate cash, and create systems that scale your business without burning you out.

This book is your roadmap. Every chapter ahead will break down the strategies, insights, and real-world examples you need to push past that $20K mark and beyond. By the end, you won't just have a thriving coaching business—you'll be a leader in your space, standing out in a sea of coaches all scrambling for attention.

So fasten your seatbelt, get ready to take action, and let's turn your coaching business into a thriving, consistent 6-figure income machine. The journey starts now.

Chapter Two

Magic Message Makeover

Standing Out In A Saturated Market

The Post That Changed Everything: A Fitness Coach's Confession

Just a few years back, I was in a tough spot. I mean, I was making money - bouncing between 5k and 15k a month - but it was a freaking rollercoaster. One month I'd be crushing it, the next I'd be sweating bullets wondering how I'd pay the bills.

I was posting content like crazy. Workouts, inspirational quotes, helpful tips - you name it, I was sharing it. And yeah, I had a decent following. People were liking my stuff.

But... likes don't pay the bills. I knew I had more potential, but something was off.

The clock was ticking. This was my only source of income, and failure wasn't an option. I had a family to support, and the thought of going back to a regular job or the gym was like a punch to the gut.

Then one morning, everything changed. I woke up, checked my phone, and BAM - hundreds of notifications. DMs flooding in like crazy. I thought my account was hacked or something.

But nope. It was just one post. One post that I didn't even think was anything special when I made it. But something about it struck a chord.

So I studied that post like it was the key to the universe. What made it different? Why did it resonate so much? And then I tried to recreate that magic.

Guess what? It worked. Again and again. In just 30 days, I closed 11 clients and made $33,383. That's when I knew I was onto something big.

I developed this posting framework that nobody else was doing. Put it into a specific format. And it just kept working. So well that other coaches started asking me, *"Dude, how are you getting all these clients?"*

That's when I realized - I had cracked the code. I called it the content conversion system. And over the next couple of years, it generated over 4000 leads, 1000+ calls, and 472 clients.

The best part? No more hustling 24/7. No more expensive ads or gimmicky tactics. Just a simple system that turned my social media into a client-attracting machine.

90 days after implementing this system, it hit me: I was never going to struggle to book calls or get clients again. As long as I had a social media account or email, I basically had a license to print money.

But the real game-changer? I went from chasing clients to having them come to me. Suddenly, I was the go-to expert. The in-demand coach I always knew I could be.

And now, I'm going to share with you the FIRST step to making this system work for you.

Your Messaging.

———————— ● ————————

The Magic of Messaging: Your Key to Attracting Dream Clients

You know what's funny? In this crazy world of online coaching, everyone's running around like a chicken with its head cut off, chasing the next big marketing hack or trying to go viral on TikTok. It's like watching squirrels on Red Bull, I swear.

But here's the cold, hard truth - that crap doesn't work. Not in the long run, anyway.

In this chapter, we're going to cut through the BS and focus on the one thing that makes ALL of your marketing work: **Your Brand Message.**

We're going to focus on nailing your messaging. Dialing in on exactly what your ideal clients need to hear to make them think, "I need to work with this coach."

This isn't about getting a celebrity shout out or going viral on Instagram. It's about laying down a foundation so solid, it'll make all of your marketing produce 10x the results (just by changing the words you use).

The #1 Truth About Online Marketing (That Nobody Wants to Admit)

Here's the deal... The #1 truth about getting more inbound DMs, booked calls, and closing more clients is this: It's not about doing MORE. It's about doing it RIGHT.

Most online coaches think they need to post more content, send more DMs, run more challenges... But you've already proven that doing more volume isn't the answer, right?

Why? Because when you're saying the wrong message to the wrong people at the wrong time, you get crickets. Or worse, you get a bunch of tire-kickers who waste your time and never buy.

Let me hit you with a real example...

I was consulting this coach a few weeks back. Dude had over 121,000 followers on Facebook. Sounds impressive, right? But guess what - he was making less than a McDonald's cook. His posts were getting massive engagement, he had plenty of "leads" to talk to. But he couldn't convert them into clients to save his life.

Now, flip that script. My client Leo has less than 3,000 friends on Facebook. But he's filling his calendar with calls and hitting $30k months. What's the difference?

One word: Messaging.

Here's the truth: The only way you're going to get the RIGHT people interested in your program is if you say the right words. You can say the wrong thing a million times to the right people, and they still won't buy. But say the RIGHT thing, in the RIGHT order, to the RIGHT people... and sales become almost effortless.

It's kinda like going to China and you're trying to order food. And you speak English. It will not work. Because they don't understand English. But if you speak Chinese, magically you can order some freakin' Chinese food.

Your marketing is no different. You have to say the right words and then plug those words into the right content.

Imagine waking up to an inbox full of inbound DMs, a calendar packed with qualified sales calls, and 2-4 perfect-fit clients enrolling each week. How would that feel?

That's what becomes possible when you nail your messaging.

But if you don't get that REFINING your messaging is the fastest way to get your content attracting more clients, you're going to stay stuck in the 'content commodity trap'. You'll be chasing leads and fighting for clients forever.

I'm not going to let that happen to you. Because the truth is, you don't need more content, more DMing, or harder work. You need the right words, said to the right people, at the right time. Get that right, and everything else falls into place.

Identifying Who Matters Most (AKA Who's Gonna Pay You)

Alright, let's break this down and get clear about who you're actually trying to help.

Because this is where most coaches screw up royally.

You can't help everyone, and you shouldn't try. That's a fast track to burnout and a business that's about as focused as a dog in a squirrel park.

So, who are you actually trying to help?

And I'm not talking about some vague BS like *"women who want to get fit."* That's not gonna cut it.

We're diving deep here. It's about understanding their fears, their dreams, the stuff that keeps them up at 3 AM staring at the ceiling.

What are they struggling with right now? What have they tried before that didn't work? What do they actually want to achieve?

When you get crystal clear on this, it's like turning on a spotlight in a dark room. Suddenly, everything in your business gets sharper.

Your marketing? It'll speak directly to your ideal client like you're reading their mind.

Your services? They'll be exactly what your people are desperate for.

I'm going to give you a framework to unpack your messaging in just a minute...

But understand this... get this right, and you'll stop wasting time on tire-kickers and start attracting people who are ready to invest in themselves and in you.

So, are you ready to get serious about who you're really here to serve? Let's dive in...

Crafting a Message That Resonates (And Actually Makes People Give a Damn)

Once you've nailed down who your ideal client is, the next step is crafting a core message that hits home. Think of this message as the heartbeat of your coaching business. It's what sets you apart in a sea of coaches. Your message needs to speak directly to your client's dreams and struggles, promising them a real, tangible transformation.

In this chapter, we'll dive into how to create a message that's not just authentic but also strategically powerful. Get ready to discover how to make your message resonate and convert like crazy.

Crafting Your Core Message (The Beating Heart of Your Biz)

Alright, let's talk about your core message. This isn't just some tagline you put in your bio... This is the beating heart of your entire coaching business.

Your core message is like planting a flag in the ground. It tells the world, *"This is who I am, this is what I stand for, and this is how I'm going to change your life."*

When you nail this, it's like a magnet for your ideal clients. It speaks to their deepest desires, their biggest fears, and makes them think, *"Holy crap, this coach gets me."*

But here's the thing - your core message isn't just about what you do. It's about the transformation you provide. It's about taking your client from where they are now (probably frustrated, stuck, and ready to give up) to where they want to be (crushing their goals and feeling like a badass).

You need to be able to communicate this in a way that's so clear, so compelling, that even your grandma could understand it. And you need to be able to do it in just a few sentences.

This isn't about being clever or cute. It's about being real. It's about digging deep into who you are, what you've been through, and how that makes you uniquely qualified to help your clients.

Ask yourself: What's the one thing I wish every single one of my clients understood about achieving their goals? That's your starting point.

Your core message should make your ideal client stop in their tracks and think, *"Dang, where has this coach been all my life?"*

So, let me ask you this: How does your core message reflect the unique transformation you provide? If you can't answer that in one sentence, you've got some work to do.

Remember, in a world where everyone's shouting for attention, a clear, powerful core message is what's going to make you stand out. It's what's going to turn tire-kickers into paying clients, and clients into raving fans.

The Magic Message Framework

Crafting the Magic Message

In today's digital world, over 600,000 posts are published every minute on the internet. Gone are the days when you could simply make an educational post and get flooded with interest. To stand out, you need to think more strategically.

The real problem isn't volume - you're probably already posting enough content or DM'ing enough people. The issue is that your content isn't speaking to your audience on a gut level. It's not making them think, *"This is for me."*

Here's the truth: You can send the wrong message a million times, but the right person will never respond. But send the right message once, and the perfect prospect will raise their hand.

The Magic Message Framework is designed to guide you through creating a message that not only captures attention but also converts prospects into loyal clients. Let's break down each element of this framework.

Magic Messaging Framework

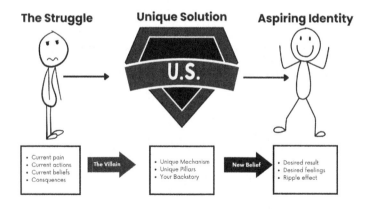

Defining Your Dream Clients (The Main Character)

The first step is to define your 'dream client' with precision. Consider their demographics, such as age and location, and their psychographics, such as values and lifestyle. Questions like *"What keeps them up at night?"* or *"What dreams do they yearn to achieve?"* help in painting a clear picture of who you are talking to.

The Struggle:

Next, identify your avatar's current pains, actions, beliefs, and consequences.

The secret here is getting specific and tangible. The more specific you get... the more effective your messaging will be.

Example:

- Current pain: Struggling to lose the last 20 lbs of belly fat despite trying various diets

- Actions: Yo-yo dieting, sporadic gym visits, skipping meals due to busy schedule

- Beliefs: *"I don't have time to eat healthy or exercise regularly"*

- Consequences: Low energy, poor self-esteem, health concerns

Action: Write the SPECIFIC pain points, actions, limiting beliefs and consequences your ideal clients have.

The Transformation

Define the specific goals, desires, results, and feelings your ideal clients want.

Again, here you'll want to get specific and speak in tangible results

Example:

- Specific goal: Lose 20 pounds in 3 months

- Desired feelings: Confident, energetic, in control

- Ripple effect: Improved work performance, better personal relationships

Action: Write out the specific goals, desires, and feeling they your ideal clients want.

The Real Cause:

Pinpoint the actual problem causing their pain (which they might not know yet).

Example: Inconsistent habits and lack of a sustainable, personalized approach to fitness and nutrition

Action: Write down the REAL cause that's keeping them stuck

The Villain:

Name the old way or misconception that's holding them back.

A villain or antagonist is part of every great story...

Think of Batman. They give the storyline villains like 'The Joker,' 'Bane,' 'The Penguin'... and they are the ones destroying Gotham.

Now, imagine if there weren't any NAMES or faces to the villains (just bad guys). It wouldn't be as interesting, right?

The Villain for you is: The misconception or outdated approach that's wreaking havoc in your clients' lives.

For instance, in the fitness world, the villain might be the *"Restricted Diet Trap"* or the *"Broken Metabolism Myth."*

It's the thing your clients believe is true, but is actually holding them back.

Action: Name the Villain (old way or misconception) holding them back.

Your Unique Solution:

Develop your process or methodology that solves their specific problem.

Your unique solution is like your superhero alter ego. It's the special combination of methods, strategies, and insights that only you can offer.

In my fitness business, it wasn't just about working out and eating right - it was the *"Flex Fuel Nutrition"* combined with *"Metabolic Intensity Training."*

It's not about reinventing the wheel, but about packaging your approach in a way that resonates with your audience and solves their specific problems.

Example:

Unique Solution: Stubborn Fat Solution - A three-step system:

1. Flex Fuel Nutrition

2. Metabolic Resistance Training

3. Mindfuel Innercises

Action: Name your unique solution (don't overthink this)

The New Belief:

Articulate why your way works and what your clients need to believe to buy in.

These are the game-changers. They're the mindset shifts that make your clients go *"Aha!"* and see their problems in a whole new light.

For example, in my fitness business, a key new belief was *"If you eat right, not just healthy, and get your calories dialed in, then you will lose belly fat."* This simple shift in thinking opened up a whole new world for my prospects and made them eager to learn more about how to implement it.

Example:

The New Belief: *"You can achieve significant weight loss and improve your health with just 30 minutes a day, even with a busy schedule."*

Action: Write the NEW belief(s) your ideal clients must believe in order to want your solution (note: this just be your truth)

The Aspiring Identity:

Define who your clients want to become.

Think of the aspiring identity as the superhero version of your client. It's who they dream of becoming when all their problems are solved and their goals are achieved. This isn't just about external changes - it's about who they become on the inside too.

In my fitness business, the aspiring identity wasn't just *"a person who lost weight."* It was *"a fit parent"* - someone who not only looked great but had the energy to play with their kids and set a healthy example for their family.

For my coaching clients, the aspiring identity is often *"the sought-after coach"* or *"the successful online entrepreneur."* It's not just about making money, but about becoming the go-to expert in their niche, the person others look up to and want to learn from.

The aspiring identity is powerful because it taps into your clients' deeper motivations. It's not just about losing 20 pounds or making $30k a month - it's about becoming the person they've always wanted to be.

When you nail this, your marketing speaks to your clients' souls.

They're not just buying a service; they're investing in becoming their ideal selves. That's why I always say, *"Your message matters now more than it ever has before."* Because when you can articulate this aspiring identity clearly, you're not just selling a product or service - you're offering a transformation.

Remember, people don't just buy what you do; they buy who they become when they work with you. Get this right, and you'll have clients lining up to work with you, ready to transform into the person they've always dreamed of being.

Example:

The Aspiring Identity: "The Fit and Focused Professional."

Action: Name their aspiring identity

Mapping Out the Unique Value Proposition

Your unique value proposition (UVP) sets you apart from the competition. Here, you define what makes your coaching approach special. Maybe it's your personal backstory, your methodology, or your specific area of expertise.

This isn't just some fancy marketing term - it's the secret sauce that makes you stand out in a sea of coaches who all sound the same.

Think of your UVP as your coaching superpower. It's what makes you the go-to expert instead of just another face in the crowd.

Now, I want you to ask yourself: *"What makes my coaching unique?"* This will help you clarify your UVP.

Maybe it's your personal story. Did you go from being a struggling overweight parent to a fit CEO? That's gold. Or maybe it's your unique methodology - like my "Flex Fuel Nutrition" or "Metabolic Intensity Training."

Here's the thing: Your UVP isn't just about being different for the sake of being different. It's about solving your clients' problems in a way that no one else can.

Remember when I talked about the coach with 121,000 followers who was making less than a McDonald's cook? That's what happens when you don't have a strong UVP. You might get likes, but you won't get clients.

On the flip side, my client Leo, with less than 3,000 Facebook friends was crushing it at $30k months. Why? Because his UVP was crystal clear and spoke directly to his ideal clients.

So, here's what I want you to do:

1. Identify what makes you unique. Is it your story, your method, or your results?

2. Figure out how this uniqueness solves your ideal client's problems.

3. Communicate this in a way that makes your ideal clients think, "Holy crap, this coach gets me!"

Remember, when you nail your UVP, you're not just another coach. You become THE coach for your ideal clients. And that, my friend, is how you become truly in-demand.

Crafting the Message

Alright, let's get down to the nitty-gritty of crafting your message. This isn't just about stringing together some fancy words. We're talking about a headline that stops people in their tracks, a story that punches them right in the feels, and a call-to-action that makes them think, *"Dang, I need this NOW."*

Your message needs to scream what you're all about and why your clients can't live without you. It's like creating a perfect cocktail - each ingredient of the Hero Message Framework needs to work together to create something that's greater than the sum of its parts.

When you nail this, you're not just marketing - you're speaking directly to your ideal client's soul. And trust me, when you get this right, it makes every other part of your business fall into place.

By weaving together all these pieces of the Magic Messaging Framework, you're setting yourself up for marketing that actually works. We're not talking

about fluffy vanity metrics here - we're talking about real, paying clients knocking down your digital door.

As we wrap this chapter up, let's get one thing straight: Going viral or being *"famous on the internet"* might give you a quick high, but it won't build a business that lasts. The real secret sauce?

Understanding your market like the back of your hand and speaking to them in a way that makes them feel seen and understood.

Let's break it down:

Step 1: Identify Your Dream Client, which involves choosing a WHO and then get crystal clear on your ideal client's pain points. What keeps them up at 3 AM? What have they tried that's failed miserably? This is about understanding their current pains, actions, beliefs, and consequences.

Step 2: Develop Empathy and Understanding You need to know your clients better than they know themselves. This is about feeling their pain, understanding their struggles, and knowing exactly what they need - even if they don't know it yet.

Step 3: Craft Your Core Message This is where you take everything from the previous steps and distill it into a message that hits like a ton of bricks. It needs to make your ideal client stop scrolling and think, *"Holy crap, this is exactly what I need."*

Step 4: Show Proof and Provide Social Proof, Talk is cheap. You need to back up your claims with real results. Testimonials, case studies, before-and-afters - whatever it takes to show that you're the real deal.

Step 5: Consistency across Platforms Your message needs to be everywhere your ideal client looks. Whether they're on Instagram, Facebook, or your website, they should hear the same powerful message.

Finally, **Step 6: Test and Refine** This isn't a *"set it and forget it"* deal. You need to constantly test, tweak, and improve your message. What worked yesterday might not work tomorrow. Your message WILL evolve over time.

BONUS: Go to www.indemandcoach.com/bookresources to download a free copy of the Magic Messaging Tool

Here's the bottom line: This isn't about being the loudest or the flashiest. It's about being the voice that speaks directly to your ideal client's deepest desires and biggest fears. Get this right, and you'll have clients lining up around the digital block to work with you.

Remember, your message matters now more than ever before. Don't be afraid to speak it. Now let's take these insights and plug them into strategic content marketing.

Chapter Three

Strategic Content Distribution

From Ignored To In-Demand

The business looked good on paper. But paper doesn't tell the whole story...

I remember sitting at my desk late one night, scrolling through my Facebook. Thousands of followers. Hundreds of likes on every post. The kind of engagement most coaches dream about.

But my bank account? It told a different story.

Sure, I was making money - somewhere between $5K and $15K most months. But it was like riding a rollercoaster blindfolded. Some months I'd be flying high, others I'd be white-knuckling it through, praying I could keep the lights on.

I was doing everything *"right."* Sharing workout videos that took hours to film. Crafting inspiring captions that would make Tony Robbins proud. Dropping value bombs like I was getting paid by the tip.

My audience was growing. People were watching. But something wasn't clicking.

The worst part? This wasn't just about me. I had a family counting on this working. The thought of crawling back to a gym job or getting into sales felt like admitting defeat. That wasn't an option.

Then came that morning. You know those moments that change everything? This was mine.

I woke up, grabbed my phone (bad habit, I know), and literally did a double-take. Hundreds of notifications. DMs pouring in like a broken faucet. My first thought? *"Great, I've been hacked."*

But it wasn't a hack. It was a post. Just one simple post I'd thrown up without much thought.

Something about it hit different. Like accidentally stumbling onto a secret frequency that everyone was tuned into.

So I did what any desperate entrepreneur would do - I turned into a mad scientist. Analyzed every word. Every phrase. Tried to reverse engineer whatever magic had just happened.

Then I tried to replicate it. And it worked. Again. And again.

30 days later, I'd signed 11 new clients and banked $33,383. From posts. Not ads. Not funnels. Not some complicated tech stack.

I'd found a pattern. A framework. Something so different from what everyone else was doing that other coaches started sliding into MY DMs asking what the hell I was doing differently.

That's when I knew I had to turn this into a real system. Something repeatable. Reliable.

I called it the Content Conversion System.

It's not sexy. It's not complicated. But it works like nothing else I've ever seen.

——————— • ———————

The Power of Strategic Content

It's time to dive deep into creating content that consistently generates leads, gets people raising their hands, responding to your calls to action, and sliding into your DMs—all without the need for endless content creation or chasing down leads in Messenger, which we all know can lead to burnout.

This chapter is designed to show you how to create content that not only engages your audience but also drives sales. The key here is to understand that strategic content is about more than just building an audience—it's about creating demand for your unique solution and shifting the perspectives of the right people. As business owners, not influencers, our primary focus is on driving results, and this module will teach you how to do just that.

Building Your Content Ecosystem

Let me walk you through my strategic content ecosystem—this has been my secret weapon for consistently and predictably generating leads and sales in my business. Over the past 12 years, I've been posting content and marketing, and there's something I've realized: information is a commodity, and content is commoditized. People don't value it like they used to. The perceived value has gone way down. Now, you still want to post content. But we have to change the narrative... to how people PERCEIVE the information.

Here's the thing – if you want to stand out and make your content work for you, you need an intentional content system designed around conversions.

Now, back in the day, I was just posting content and hoping the value I provided was enough to get people interested and asking for help. And to be fair, that worked for a while, especially around 2016-2018. But then 2020 hit, and suddenly, millions—if not billions—of people flooded online, posting content, starting businesses, and competing for attention. The landscape changed, and so did the need for a more systematic approach.

This content ecosystem I'm about to share with you isn't just about throwing content out there and crossing your fingers. It's about creating a structured, intentional system that attracts, nurtures, and converts.

First things first, we need to set up your content ecosystem. This isn't about being everywhere - it's about being strategic. Here's the trifecta that's going to transform your business:

Top of Funnel Platform: This is your main stage. Choose one - Facebook, Instagram, or LinkedIn. Don't try to be everywhere. Master one platform and dominate it.

Email: This is your nurture channel. It's where you build deeper relationships with your audience and guide them towards your offers.

YouTube: This is your long-form content hub. It's where you establish your authority and give your audience a chance to binge on your content. Most coaches struggle with inbound leads because they focus too much on short-form content (reels, posts). While great for attention, it takes many 30-second clips and written posts to build enough trust for high-ticket sales.

Long-form content is the key to building deep trust and attracting high-paying clients... and YouTube is a highly effective way to do that.

Now, I know what you're thinking. *"Jason, that sounds like a lot."* But here's the secret: you don't need to create separate content for each platform. Repurpose, my friend. Repurpose.

For example, you can take your YouTube video, strip the audio for a podcast, and use the transcript of the video to write a post for your social media content. Work smarter, not harder.

Creating Your Content Cadence

Alright, now that we've got your ecosystem set up, let's talk about what kind of content you're going to pump through it. We're going to focus on four main types of content:

1. Connection Content

This is where you show your human side. Share your lifestyle, your values, your beliefs. Talk about your deeper purpose. Why do you do what you do? This isn't about your business - it's about you as a person.

For example, I might share a post about my philosophy: *"If you focus on being in demand, the money and things will follow."* This kind of content builds a deeper connection with your audience. They start to see you as a real person, not just another faceless brand.

2. Influence Content

This is where you start shifting perspectives. You're not just teaching - you're changing how your audience thinks about their problems and solutions.

Break down common misconceptions. Dismantle objections. Show them why their current approach isn't working. This is where you position yourself as a thought leader, not just another coach regurgitating the same old advice.

3. Authority Content

This is where you flex your expertise. But here's the key: don't just give them vitamins, give them painkillers. What do I mean by that? Don't just share generic "how-to" information. Give them specific, actionable insights and "lightbulb moments" that solve their immediate pain points.

For instance, instead of just saying "eat a calorie deficit," you might say, *"Here's the difference between eating healthy and eating right."* See the difference? You're not just sharing information - you're giving them an "aha" moment.

4. Conversion Content

This is where you systematically generate inbound leads and convert. It's content designed to drive action - whether that's getting them to raise their hand, book a call, or buy your offer.

This could be things like "CTA" posts, live trainings, or mini VSLs (video sales letters). The key here is to be strategic. Don't just throw out random calls to action. Build up to them with your other content types.

Running Conversion Content Campaigns

Now, here's where we take things to the next level. Instead of just randomly posting content and hoping for the best, we're going to run intentional 'conversion content campaigns'.

Most business owners 'post & pray' that their content will land them red-hot leads... but have no REAL method behind their madness.

If you want inbound leads DM'ing you, clicking links in your emails, or opting into your lead magnets...

... you need a system for making that happen (at least consistently)

A 'conversion content campaign' is a focused sequence of content designed to guide your audience towards a specific conversion event. This could be a live training, a workshop, or even a program launch.

Think of it like a NARRATIVE. Your content becomes almost like a storyline leading your audience from step to step.

Here's how it works:

1. **Choose a Theme**: Start with a specific pain point or desire from your messaging. For example, "booking more consistent sales calls."

2. **Create a Hook**: This is your attention-grabber. Make it polarizing. For instance: *"How to book 10 sales calls a week without spending a dime on ads."*

3. **Map Out Your Sequence**: This could be a series of posts leading up to your main event. Maybe a *"hand raiser"* post, followed by a teaser, then your main training.

4. **Add Supporting Content**: Sprinkle in some of your regular content (connection, influence, authority) that ties into your theme.

5. **Follow Up**: Don't just drop the ball after your event. Follow up with everyone who engaged. Send personal messages. Keep nurturing those leads.

The beauty of this system is that it creates predictability. You're not just throwing content out there and hoping something sticks. You're strategically guiding your audience through a journey that ends with them wanting what you're offering.

Remember, the key to making this work is consistency and analysis. Track your KPIs religiously. Look at your engagement rates, your conversion rates, your sales. The numbers don't lie. Use them to constantly refine and improve your approach.

And here's a pro tip: don't be afraid to rinse and repeat. Once you find a campaign that works well, don't just use it once. Run it again in a few months. Tweak it, improve it, but don't reinvent the wheel every time.

Real-World Impact: A Case Study

Let me share a quick success story to show you just how powerful this system can be. Take my client Leo, a health coach. Leo had hit some $8k-$12k/m's but was struggling to scale past that... not to mention, he was pushing HARD just to get to $10k/m's... his income was unstable, which made him feel insanely stressed. He couldn't even be present with his kids... because he was worried about money and getting clients.

He had tried growing a FB group, DMing everyone who engaged with his content, running ads and even hiring "experts", yet he still was fighting tooth & nail to keep his sales calls booked on his calendar.

But he applied the strategies in the strategic content ecosystem and on month 2 of applying this he had $16,798 but it gets even better. In his 3rd month he made $33,174 and in his 4th month he made $38,172... He didn't send a

SINGLE outbound DM, run a single ad. All of this came from inbound traffic from the process just outlined above.

Chapter Four

The Value-First Funnel

Attracting High-Paying Dream Clients with T-Shape Workshops

Divine Intervention or Dumb Luck?

I accidentally stumbled upon this unorthodox strategy. Let me take you back to 2019. I was running a gym, knew I was going to sell it soon, and was starting to dip my toes into the online space. But here's the thing - I wasn't really creating much content at the time.

I had a few people interested in buying the gym - folks from New York, Jersey, a couple of locals. But I wasn't putting myself out there much. I was building an online program on the side, but content creation? Not really my focus.

Then, call it divine intervention or just dumb luck, something told me to start pumping out more content. So I did. And then, boom - COVID hit. Suddenly, nobody wanted to buy a brick-and-mortar gym. Talk about timing, right?

But here's where it gets interesting. For the next year and a half, maybe two years, I went all in on content. I'm talking live videos every single day. Challenges, workshops, you name it. I was creating content like my life depended on it.

Fast forward a bit, and I've built up a decent following. We're talking 8 to 10,000 people. Not too shabby, right? But here's the thing - I was still bouncing between $10k and $20k months. The lead flow was there, but the conversions? Not so much.

I was getting hundreds of likes, tons of engagement, but it wasn't translating to sales. I was scratching my head, wondering what the hell I was doing wrong.

Then one day, it happened. I made this post on Facebook - nothing special, just another day, another piece of content. But the next morning, I woke up to a flood of notifications. We're talking 13 or 14 inbound leads from quality people sliding into my DMs.

I was floored. What had I done differently? I started studying that post, trying to reverse engineer what made it work. And that's when it hit me - it wasn't about how much content I was creating. It was about how I was shifting people's beliefs and positioning my unique IP.

That's when I discovered the power of what I now call the Value-First Funnel. It wasn't about pumping out endless content and praying for results. It was about strategically crafting content that shifted perspectives, solved specific problems, and naturally led people to want more.

From that moment on, I stopped playing the quantity game and started focusing on quality. I developed the T-shape workshop strategy, fine-tuned my messaging, and boom - suddenly, I was consistently hitting those $30k months, then $50k, and beyond.

And the best part? It felt effortless. No more grinding out endless content. No more hoping and praying for leads. Just a steady stream of high-quality, ready-to-buy clients knocking at my digital door.

That's the power of the Value-First Funnel, folks. And that's what I'm going to teach you in this chapter. So get ready, because we're about to transform the way you attract clients forever.

———————— ● ————————

Okay, I'm just going to come right out and say it.

It's time to ditch the spray-and-pray approach and get strategic about attracting those high-paying dream clients. I'm talking about the ones who light you up, get amazing results, and remind you why you got into this game in the first place.

Let's face it – we've all had those clients that make us want to pull our hair out. They're not the right fit, they don't vibe with our values, and working with them feels like pulling teeth. But what if I told you there's a way to filter out those low-quality leads and bring in the cream of the crop?

Enter the Value-First Funnel system. This isn't just another lead generation strategy. It's a lead nurture strategy that'll have clients knocking down your virtual door without you having to slide into a single DM.

Now, I know what you're thinking. "Jason, I've tried everything. Free stuff, challenges, lead magnets – the works." But here's the deal: the old way of getting clients is dead. We're living in a different era now, and if you want to stand out, you've got to level up your game.

———————— • ————————

The Problem with the Old Way

Let's break down why the old approach just doesn't cut it anymore:

1. Long buying cycles

2. High-pressure sales (yuck)

3. Few leads actually buy (we're talking 3-5% if you're lucky)

4. Most leads die in your funnel unless you've got a killer follow-up process

It's a constant cycle of chasing new leads, and let's be honest – it's exhausting.

The New Way: Short Form to Long Form to T-Shape Workshops

Here's the secret sauce:

1. Short-form content (think social media posts, reels)

2. Long-form content (newsletters, podcasts, YouTube videos)

3. T-shape workshops

4. Higher ticket offers

This approach builds trust faster, increases the right kind of engagement, and makes high-ticket sales a breeze. Plus, there's no cold DMing or pushy sales tactics. It's all about creating a journey of smaller yeses that lead to bigger yeses.

The Long-Form Secret

Here's where most coaches drop the ball: they focus too much on short-form content. Sure, those 30-second reels might get you some attention, but it takes a lot of those to build enough trust for someone to whip out their credit card for your high-ticket offer.

Long-form content is the key to building deep trust and attracting those high-paying clients. And the T-shape workshop strategy? It's the secret weapon in leveraging that long-form content.

The T-Shape Workshop Strategy

Imagine this for a sec: you take your intellectual property – all those pillars and phases you teach – and break it down into bite-sized, problem-solving workshops. We're talking laser-focused, deep-dive sessions that tackle one specific issue your ideal clients are facing.

For example, let's say you've got a system with three main pillars: magic messaging makeovers, conversion content cadence, and value-first conversion systems (those are mine). Instead of trying to cram all that into one workshop, you'd pick one sliver – like crafting killer hooks – and go deep on that.

The beauty of this approach? It gives potential clients a taste of your coaching style, helps them get real results, and leaves them hungry for more. It's like giving them the appetizer that makes them crave the full-course meal.

T-Shape Workshops™

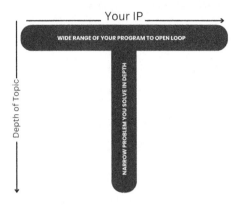

Crafting Your T-Shape Workshop

Here's how to make this work:

1. Choose a narrow, specific problem to solve

2. Go deep on that one issue

3. Deliver real, actionable value

4. Open loop to your broader offerings

Remember, this isn't about overwhelming people with information or trying to teach them everything you know in one go. It's about solving a specific problem in a complete way, while hinting at the bigger picture.

The Secret Ingredient: Open Loops

Here's where the magic happens. Throughout your workshop, you want to sprinkle in hints about your broader offerings. Talk about client results from your full program. Mention other aspects of your system that tie into the topic at hand. It's like leaving breadcrumbs that lead them to your higher-ticket offers.

The key is to make it natural. You're not here to do a hard sell. You're here to genuinely help people and show them what's possible when they work with you.

Promoting Your Workshop

Now, let's talk about getting butts in seats (or eyes on screens, as it were). The promotional strategy is crucial, and it's where most coaches drop the ball. Here's the framework I swear by:

1. Whisper (6-7 days out): Start planting seeds with questions and polls.

2. Tease (3-5 days out): Drop some promotional posts, belief shifters, and social proof.

3. Shout (1-2 days out): Hit them with the

FOMO-style posts.

And remember, it's not just about social media. Leverage your email list, partnerships, and client referrals. The key is to create urgency and demand without being pushy.

Making It Evergreen

Here's where you really start to scale. Once you've run your live workshop, turn it into an evergreen asset. List it for sale on your website, add it as a PS in your emails, or use it as a bonus in future promotions. The goal is to see it as an asset that keeps working for you long after the live event is over.

The Bottom Line

Listen, this Value-First Funnel system isn't just about making more money (although that's a nice side effect). It's about attracting the right clients – the ones who value what you do, get amazing results, and make you love your job even more.

It's about being a coach first and a marketer second. It's about creating a system that brings clients to you, instead of you chasing after them. And most importantly, it's about delivering real value that changes lives.

So, are you ready to ditch the old way and embrace the Value-First Funnel? Trust me, your future high-paying dream clients are waiting. It's time to give them what they want – and what they need.

Now get out there and start planning your first T-shape workshop. Your business (and your sanity) will thank you.

Chapter Five

From Prospect to Client

Cash Conversion Blueprint

I Stole the Sales Manual from LA Fitness... and It Changed Everything.

This is pretty embarrassing, I gotta admit. But picture this: Me, a rookie personal trainer, busting my butt for 12-15 hours a day, making a measly $6 for every 25-minute session. Meanwhile, LA Fitness? They're pocketing $54 per session. Talk about getting the short end of the stick, right?

Now, don't get me wrong. I was grateful for the job. It was my training ground. But let's be real: I could barely afford ramen noodles, let alone rent.

Every day, I'd watch Tony, the PT sales manager, closing deals left and right like it was breathing. Sales? I wanted NOTHING to do with it. But here's the thing - I knew if I wanted to eat something other than noodles, I had to get good at it. Fast.

So, I planted myself in the corner between sessions, nose buried in the company's sales manual. Read it front to back, again and again. Then came the day I made a decision that would change everything. I decided to... shall we say... "permanently borrow" that manual.

Ethical? Debatable. Worth it? Absolutely.

I spent nights rewriting every word into a Google doc, burning that sales process into my brain. It felt like downloading a new skill set, *"Matrix"* style.

A week later, BAM! I landed my first $1000/hr client. My palms were sweaty, but those sales techniques? They worked like a charm.

Two months in, I'm bringing home $8,000 a month. And nope, not a dime from LA Fitness payroll.

But why stop there?

Riding that motivation high, I dove headfirst into studying marketing. Blog posts, videos, books - you name it, I devoured it.

3 months later, I filled a bootcamp in a local park with 50 members. Suddenly, I'm looking at $12,500 a month. Not bad for a guy who could barely afford rent, huh?

It wasn't all smooth sailing. There were doubts, setbacks, moments when I wondered if I was in over my head. But I kept at it. Day after day... study, sweat, sell... repeat.

Seven months and 89 clients later, I took the biggest leap yet: I decided to start my own gym.

Looking back, *"borrowing"* that manual was a turning point. It taught me that success leaves clues - if you're willing to look for them and put in the work.

Fast forward to today, 6000+ leads, 1000+ sales consults, 500+ clients... all from learning money-making skills and building systems to make sales repeatable.

The moral of the story? It's not about working harder. It's about working smarter. It's about finding the right message, the right system, and then leveraging the heck out of it.

So, are you ready to stop spinning your wheels and start building a real, profitable coaching business? Let's dive in and turn your messaging into a client-attracting machine.

———————— • ————————

Building a Cash Conversion Machine

The path to consistent, scalable revenue in any coaching business lies in building a Cash Conversion Machine—a system designed to attract, nurture, and convert leads into paying clients efficiently and predictably. In this chapter, we'll break down the essential components of this machine, so you can start seeing results without relying on constant manual outreach or the exhausting grind of one-on-one interactions.

The goal here is simple: to create a system that does the heavy lifting for you, allowing you to focus on delivering your best work while your pipeline fills up with high-quality leads ready to invest in your services.

Effective Lead Nurture Systems

At the heart of any successful Cash Conversion Machine is an effective lead nurture system. This is where the magic happens—where cold prospects transform into warm leads, and eventually, into loyal clients. But nurturing leads isn't about sending generic follow-up emails or bombarding your list with sales pitches. It's about creating meaningful connections and providing value that positions you as the go-to authority in your niche.

To nurture leads effectively, you need to establish a system that consistently engages your audience with strategic content and personal interactions. Here's how you can do it:

1. **Build a Pipeline**: Your pipeline is the lifeblood of your business. It's the pool of potential clients who have shown interest in what you offer but haven't yet taken the plunge. Building a pipeline of red-hot 'dream clients' means consistently adding new leads, whether through organic strategies like content marketing or paid advertising. But it doesn't stop there—once leads are in your pipeline, you need a plan to move them toward conversion.

2. **Have a Connection Block**: A Connection Block is a dedicated time in your schedule where you focus solely on building and strengthening relationships with people in your pipeline. This could involve commenting on their social media posts, sending personalized messages, or even hopping on a quick call to offer some free advice. The goal is to show genuine interest in their challenges and offer valuable insights, without immediately pushing for a sale. This builds trust and positions you as someone who genuinely cares about their success.

Nurture Through Strategic Content

Content is king, but not just any content—strategic content that speaks directly to the needs, desires, and pain points of your audience. The key to nurturing leads through content is to deliver value that moves them closer to making a decision to work with you. We spoke earlier about the power of LONG-FORM content...

Here's a few ways you can strategically nurture your pipeline:

1. **Mini-VSL (Video Sales Letter)**: This is your secret weapon. A short, punchy video that hits your lead's pain points, shifts their limiting beliefs, and offers a solution. It's not about selling (yet). It's about building trust and positioning yourself as the go-to expert. Unlike a full-length VSL, a Mini-VSL is designed to be consumed quickly (10-25 minutes), making it perfect for busy prospects who need a clear reason to take the next step.

2. **Trainings**: Offering free or low-cost trainings is an amazing way to nurture leads while positioning yourself as an authority in your niche. You can deliver these through live webinars, pre-recorded videos, or even as part of an email series. The goal is to give them actionable insights that your audience can implement immediately, which builds trust and keeps them engaged with your content.

3. **Workshops**: Workshops are a more interactive and intensive form of content delivery, ideal for moving warm leads closer to conversion. By offering a deep dive into a specific topic, you can jam on your audience's challenges head-on

and give ultra-specific solutions. Workshops also give you the opportunity to interact directly with participants, answer their questions, and build a stronger connection—all of which contribute to higher conversion rates.

Booking Calls & Making Sales in Mass

Once your leads have been nurtured, it's time to convert them into clients. The traditional method of booking calls and closing deals one-on-one can be time-consuming and exhausting. But there's a better way—scaling your sales process through live events that allow you to make offers to multiple people at once (spoiler: you can follow the T-Shape Workshop strategy I gave you). But here are some different ways it can look for you:

1. **Using Live Trainings**: Live trainings are an excellent way to build rapport with your audience while delivering value at scale. By positioning your training as a must-attend event, you can attract a large number of prospects who are interested in what you have to offer. These are your bread and butter. Get people on live, deliver massive value, and then make them an offer they

can't refuse. I'm talking 50, 100, even 200 people at a time.

2. **Masterclasses**: A masterclass is a more in-depth version of a live training, where you dive deep into a specific subject. These are typically longer and more comprehensive, allowing you to showcase your expertise in a way that builds significant trust with your audience. Masterclasses work particularly well for high-ticket offers, as they give you the time and space to fully explain the value of what you're selling and handle any objections on the spot.

3. **Low Ticket Workshops**: This is my secret sauce. Offer a low-priced workshop that delivers insane value. Not only does this bring in some quick cash, but it also identifies your most serious prospects. These are the people who are ready to invest in themselves. These workshops also serve as a paid lead magnet, attracting high-caliber people. The key is to deliver such immense value during the workshop that attendees are eager to take the next step with you, whether that's booking a call or enrolling in your higher-ticket programs.

Scaling Your Sales Without the Grind

The beauty of this approach is that it allows you to scale your sales process without the relentless grind of manual outreach. By leveraging live trainings, masterclasses, and workshops, you can reach more people in less time, all while delivering immense value that naturally leads to conversions.

The combination of a well-nurtured pipeline, strategic content, and scalable sales events creates a Cash Conversion Machine that works for you, even when you're not actively selling. It's about working smarter, not harder, and building a business that consistently generates revenue while giving you the freedom to focus on what you do best—helping your clients achieve their goals.

The Cash Conversion Blueprint

The first step in building your Cash Conversion Machine is developing a system that consistently attracts and nurtures leads. This starts by creating a **lead nurture system** that guides your prospects from cold leads to warm, engaged followers who are ready to invest in your services. The system must be strategic—no more sending generic messages or relying on sporadic content. The goal is to create meaningful connections that establish you as the go-to expert in your niche.

Once you've established a lead nurturing system, the next focus is on **building your pipeline**. This involves consistently adding new prospects through methods like content marketing, networking, etc. But it doesn't stop there. The real magic happens when you have a clear process for moving these leads from interested to invested. The goal is to have a steady flow of high-quality prospects who are primed to convert.

A crucial part of this machine is blocking out time specifically for **Connection Blocks**. These are dedicated moments where you focus on building relationships—commenting on posts, sending personal messages to your *"hot list,"* or jumping on calls to offer value without pushing a sale. The purpose here is to build relationships, establish trust, and show your audience you genuinely care about their success.

Next, you'll use **strategic content** to further nurture your audience. This content isn't just about posting for the sake of it—each piece serves a purpose. Whether it's a **Mini-VSL** (Video Sales Letter) or a **training**, your content should speak directly to your audience's pain points, offer solutions, and position you as the authority they need to follow. This allows your audience to see you as their go-to person for results.

As your pipeline heats up, it's time to start **booking calls and making sales at scale**. Instead of relying solely on one-on-one calls, leverage **live trainings** and **masterclasses** to convert multiple leads at once. These sessions give you a chance to deliver massive value, handle objections, and present an irresistible offer—all in front of a captivated audience. Whether you're selling through a **low-ticket workshop** or making an offer during a live training, the key is to create an environment where prospects feel ready to take action.

By combining these elements—effective nurturing, strategic content, and scalable sales—you'll build a Cash Conversion Machine that works for you, even when you're not actively selling. This approach not only increases your revenue but also gives you the freedom to focus on what you do best: delivering results for your clients.

Actionable Steps:

1. **Set up a Lead Nurture System**: Develop a process for consistently engaging your leads with valuable content and personal touchpoints.

2. **Build and Maintain Your Pipeline**: Use organic strategies and paid ads to consistently add leads to your pipeline, and implement a clear path to conversion.

3. **Create Strategic Content**: Craft Mini-VSLs, live trainings, and workshops that speak directly to your audience's pain points and offer solutions that position you as an authority.

4. **Scale Your Sales**: Use live trainings, masterclasses, and workshops to convert multiple leads at once, making your sales process more efficient.

5. **Automate for Consistency**: Ensure your Cash Conversion Machine runs smoothly with automation tools, allowing you to scale without sacrificing personal connection.

By following these steps, you'll build a system that generates revenue consistently, leaving you with more time to focus on helping your clients achieve their goals while scaling your business with ease.

Chapter Six

Buying Back Your Time

Buying Back Your Time: The Ultimate Luxury

Let me tell you a story about the day I realized time was my most valuable asset...

It was a Tuesday, around 6 PM. I was hunched over my laptop, eyes burning, chugging an energy drink. The blue light of the screen was the only thing illuminating my cramped home office.

I had just finished a grueling 14-hour workday, juggling client calls, content creation, and endless email threads. My business was growing, sure, but at what cost?

My wife and kids were in the dining room eating dinner... probably wondering if I'd ever join them. My daughter's school play? Missed it. That massage session I promised myself? Ha! A distant memory.

As I rubbed my tired eyes, a notification popped up on my phone. It was a reminder for my son's parent-teacher conference the next day. My stomach sank. I had completely forgotten about it.

That's when it hit me like a ton of bricks: I was time broke.

Sure, money was flowing in. But what good was a fat bank account if I couldn't enjoy a single minute of my day? If I was missing out on the moments that really mattered?

I realized I had fallen into the classic entrepreneur's trap. I was trading all my time for money, thinking that's what success looked like. But let me tell you something, my friend...

That ain't success. That's a hamster wheel.

Right then and there, at 6:09 PM on a Tuesday evening, I made a decision. I was going to buy back my time. I was going to build a business that served my life, not the other way around.

And you know what? It was the best damn decision I ever made.

In this chapter, I'm going to show you exactly how I did it. How I went from working 80-hour weeks to running a thriving business in just 25 hours a week. How I reclaimed my life, my health, and my relationships.

Because here's the truth: Time is the only resource you can't make more of. You can always make more money, but you can't create more time.

———————— • ————————

Reclaim Your Most Valuable Asset: Time

Alright, let's get real for a second. If you're like most coaches I've worked with, you're probably drowning in a sea of to-do lists, wearing all the hats in your business, and wondering when you'll finally have time to, you know, actually live your life. Sound familiar? Well, Well, put on your big boy (or girl) pants, because we're about to change all that.

Welcome to the chapter where we talk about buying back your time. No, I'm not selling you a time machine (though that would be pretty sweet). I'm talking about implementing systems, delegating like a boss, and using tools that'll make you wonder how you ever survived without them.

In Demand CEO Workflow

First things first - it's time to start thinking like a CEO, not a frazzled solopreneur. Here's the cold, hard truth: if you're still trying to do everything yourself, you're not just hurting your business, you're robbing yourself of the freedom you got into this game for in the first place.

So, what does an In Demand CEO workflow look like? Let me break it down for you:

1. **Prioritize like your business depends on it (because it does):** Start each week by identifying your high-impact activities. These are the 3-5 things that directly contribute to your bottom line or significantly move your business forward. Everything else? It can wait, be delegated, or maybe doesn't need to be done at all.

2. **Time block like a pro:** I'm not talking about cramming every minute of your day with tasks.

I'm talking about creating dedicated blocks for your high-impact activities, client work, and yes, even time for yourself. And here's the kicker - treat these blocks like non-negotiable appointments.

3. **Implement the "touch it once" rule:** When you open an email, deal with it right then and there. Don't leave it lingering in your inbox like a bad smell. Same goes for messages, tasks, whatever. Handle it, delegate it, or delete it. No more half-finished tasks cluttering up your mental space.

4. **Master the art of the power hour:** Set aside one hour each day for all those little tasks that always seem to pile up. Knock 'em out rapid-fire style, then move on with your day. You'll be amazed at how much you can accomplish in just 60 focused minutes.

Delegating and Outsourcing

Now, let's talk about every control freak's nightmare - letting other people do stuff in your business. I get it. Your business is your baby. But here's the thing - even babies need a village.

Here's how to start delegating like a boss:

1. **Identify your $10K/hour activities:** These are the things only you can do - the stuff that directly uses your unique skills and drives major results for your business. Everything else? Prime candidates for delegation.

2. **Start small:** You don't have to hand over the keys to your kingdom overnight. Start by outsourcing simple, repetitive tasks. Social media scheduling, email management, basic customer service - these are all great places to start.

3. **Document your processes:** Before you can hand off tasks, you need to know exactly how you do them. Create standard operating procedures (SOPs) for everything. Yes, it's a pain in the ass upfront, but trust me, it'll save you countless headaches down the road.

4. **Hire slow, fire fast:** Take your time finding the right people to support your business. But if someone isn't working out, don't drag your feet. The cost of keeping the wrong person far outweighs the discomfort of letting them go.

5. **Trust, but verify:** Once you've delegated a task, resist the urge to micromanage. Set clear expectations, then let your team do their thing. But do implement systems to check their work, especially in the beginning.

Tools for Efficiency

Alright, time for the fun part - the tools that'll make you feel like you've got a team of ninjas working behind the scenes. Here are my ride-or-die tools for maximum efficiency:

1. **Trello or Airtable (is what we use):** Project management tools that'll make you wonder how you ever managed without them. Perfect for keeping track of tasks, collaborating with your team, and making sure nothing falls through the cracks.

2. **Loom:** This screen recording tool is a game-changer for creating quick tutorials or explaining complex ideas to your team or clients. Plus, it saves you from endless back-and-forth emails.

3. **Calendly:** Say goodbye to the *"when are you free?"* email tennis. This scheduling tool integrates with your calendar and lets people book time with you hassle-free.

4. **Zapier:** The ultimate automation tool. It connects your apps and automates workflows. Once you start *"Zapping,"* you'll be addicted to finding new ways to automate your business.

5. **LastPass:** Because trying to remember a million passwords is for chumps. This password manager keeps all your login info secure and accessible.

Remember, the goal here isn't to add a bunch of fancy tools to your tech stack just for the hell of it. It's about finding the right tools that'll help you streamline your workflow and free up your time for the things that really matter.

Look, at the end of the day, buying back your time isn't just about being more efficient or making more money (though those are pretty sweet side effects). It's about creating a business that serves your life, not the other way around.

It's about being able to take a random Wednesday off to hang with your kids without your business falling apart. It's about finally booking that vacation without your laptop tagging along like an unwanted third wheel. It's about building something sustainable that doesn't require you to be chained to your desk 24/7.

So, what are you waiting for? It's time to stop being a slave to your business and start being the CEO you were meant to be. Implement these strategies, embrace delegation, and let these tools do the heavy lifting. Your future self (and your sanity) will thank you.

Action Steps: Your 7-Day Time-Buying Challenge

Okay, enough talk. It's time to put this stuff into action. Here's your 7-day challenge to start buying back your time:

Day 1: CEO Mindset Reset

- Write down your top 3 $10K/hour activities - the stuff only you can do.

- Identify 5 tasks you're currently doing that aren't on that list. These are your delegation candidates.

Day 2: Workflow Overhaul

- Set up your calendar for next week, blocking out time for your high-impact activities.

- Implement the *"touch it once"* rule. Start with your email - aim for inbox zero by end of day.

Day 3: Delegation Deep Dive

- Choose one task from your Day 1 list to delegate.

- Create a basic SOP for this task. Don't overthink it - even a quick Loom video will do.

Day 4: Tool Time

- Sign up for one new efficiency tool (Asana, Loom, Calendly, etc.).

- Spend 30 minutes learning the basics and setting it up for your needs.

Day 5: Hire Help

- Post a job listing for a virtual assistant or your first team member.

- If you already have a team, identify one new task

you can take off your plate and delegate.

Day 6: Power Hour

- Implement your first power hour. Set a timer for 60 minutes and blitz through those small tasks.

- At the end, note how many tasks you completed. This is your new benchmark.

Day 7: Reflect and Refine

- Review your week. What worked? What didn't?

- Create a plan to implement your most effective strategies permanently.

Bonus Challenge: Book that vacation you've been putting off. Yes, right now. I'll wait.

Remember, buying back your time isn't a one-and-done deal. It's a constant process of evaluating, delegating, and refining. But stick with it, and I promise you'll start seeing results faster than you can say *"virtual assistant."*

Now, get to it. Time waits for no one, but with these strategies, you'll be the one in control. Let's turn that time-strapped coach into the CEO you were meant to be. Your future self is counting on you.

Chapter Seven

Strategic Scaling for Maximum Impact

Strategic Scaling: Growing Your Business Without Losing Your Mind

Okay, I want you to picture this moment in time... It's 2019, and I'm sitting in my makeshift office (aka my kitchen table), staring at my laptop in disbelief.

My online fitness coaching business had just hit six figures. I should've been over the moon, right? But instead, I felt like I was drowning.

My inbox was overflowing. My social media was a mess. I was juggling more clients than I could handle, and the quality of my coaching was starting to slip. I hadn't seen the inside of a gym in weeks, which is pretty ironic for a fitness coach.

I remember thinking, "If this is what success looks like, I'm not sure I want it."

That night, I couldn't sleep. I tossed and turned, my mind racing with a million thoughts. How could I keep growing without burning out? How could I help more people without sacrificing the quality of my coaching? How could I scale my impact without scaling my stress?

At 4 AM, I stumbled to the kitchen for a glass of water. As I stood there in the dark, it hit me: I wasn't really scaling my business. I was just working harder, not smarter.

I had fallen into the classic trap of linear growth. More clients meant more work. More work meant less time. Less time meant more stress. It was a vicious cycle, and I was stuck in the middle of it.

Right there, in my kitchen at 4 AM, I made a decision. I was going to figure out how to scale strategically. I was going to build systems, leverage technology, and create processes that would allow me to grow my business exponentially, not just incrementally.

The next morning, I got to work. I started researching, learning, and implementing. I made mistakes, sure. But with each misstep, I learned something valuable.

Fast forward to today, and my business has grown tenfold. But here's the thing - I'm working less than I did back then. I'm helping more people, making a bigger impact, and enjoying my life in the process.

That, my friend, is the power of strategic scaling.

In this chapter, I'm going to share with you the exact strategies I used to transform my business. We're going to dive deep into the art and science of scaling smartly. You'll learn how to build systems that work for you, how to leverage technology to multiply your efforts, and how to create processes that allow your business to thrive - with or without you.

Because here's the truth: Scaling isn't just about making more money. It's about creating a business that serves your life, not consumes it. It's about growing your impact without sacrificing your sanity.

So, are you ready to leave behind the hustle and grind mentality and embrace strategic scaling? Are you ready to build a business that grows exponentially while giving you the freedom you dreamed of when you first started?

———————— • ————————

Scaling Smart: How to Grow Your Coaching Business for Maximum Impact

Alright, it's time to talk about the S-word. No, not that one—I'm talking about scaling. If you're still trading time for money, working yourself to the bone, and wondering how the hell you're going to grow without cloning yourself, this chapter's for you.

Let's get one thing straight: scaling isn't about working harder. It's about working smarter. It's about building systems that work for you, even when you're catching Z's or sipping margaritas on a beach somewhere. Sound good? Let's dive in.

Scaling Your Business Model with Systems

First things first—if you want to scale, you need systems. And I'm not talking about some fancy, complicated processes that'll make your head spin. I'm talking about simple, repeatable actions that get results. Here's how to systemize your way to success:

1. **Document Everything:** I know, I know. It sounds about as exciting as watching paint dry. But trust me on this. Start by writing down everything you do in your business. And I mean everything. From how you onboard clients to how you make your morning coffee. This is your business bible.

2. **Identify Your Money Makers:** Look at your services. Which ones are bringing in the most cash with the least effort? These are your scaling goldmines. Focus on systematizing these first.

3. **Create SOPs (Standard Operating Procedures):** For each key process in your business, create a step-by-step guide. Use videos, screenshots, whatever it takes. The goal is to make it so simple, a monkey could do it. (No offense to monkeys.)

4. **Automate What You Can:** If a task is repetitive and doesn't require your personal touch, automate it. Use tools like Zapier,

ActiveCampaign, or whatever floats your boat. The less you have to manually do, the more you can scale.

5. **Test and Refine:** Your systems aren't set in stone. Constantly test and tweak them. What's working? What's not? Be ruthless in your optimization.

Remember, the goal here is to create a business that can run without you being chained to your desk 24/7. Your systems should be your employee of the month, every month.

Expanding Your Reach

Now that you've got your systems in place, it's time to cast a wider net. But here's the kicker—we're not talking about hustling harder to reach more people. We're talking about leveraging what you've already got to multiply your impact. Here's how:

1. **Repurpose Like a Boss:** That killer Facebook post you wrote? Turn it into a video. That podcast episode? Make it a series of social media posts. Squeeze every last drop of value out of your

content.

2. **Collaborate and Conquer:** Find other coaches or businesses in complementary niches. Guest on their podcasts, do joint webinars, cross-promote. It's like borrowing someone else's audience, but in a totally non-creepy way.

3. **Leverage Paid Advertising**: Once you've got a system that converts, it's time to pour some gas on the fire. Start with a small budget and scale up as you see results. Remember, if you can put a dollar in and get two dollars out, you've got a money-printing machine.

4. **Create a Referral System:** Your happy clients are your best marketers. Create a simple, systematic way for them to refer others to you. Maybe it's a reward program, or maybe it's just making it dead easy for them to sing your praises.

5. **Go Omnichannel:** Don't put all your eggs in one basket. Spread your message across multiple platforms. But here's the key—use your systems to manage this without driving yourself crazy.

The name of the game here is leverage. How can you reach more people without proportionally increasing your workload? That's the scaling sweet spot.

Building a Team

Listen up, because this is where a lot of coaches trip up. You can't do it all alone. I don't care how smart, talented, or caffeinated you are. At some point, you need to build a team. Here's how to do it without losing your mind (or your shirt):

1. **Start with Your Weaknesses:** What tasks do you dread? What are you honestly not that great at? These are prime candidates for your first hires.

2. **Hire for Culture, Train for Skill:** You can teach someone how to use a CRM. You can't teach them not to be a jerk. Hire people who align with your values and vision.

3. **Use Project-Based Hiring First:** Before you commit to full-time employees, test the waters with project-based freelancers. Sites like Upwork or Fiverr can be gold mines for talent.

4. **Create a Solid Onboarding Process:**

Remember those SOPs you created? They're about to become your new hire's best friend. Have a clear, systematic way to bring new team members up to speed.

5. **Learn to Let Go:** This is the hardest part for many coaches. You need to trust your team to do their jobs. Micromanaging is the enemy of scaling.

6. **Invest in Team Development:** Your team is only as strong as its weakest link. Invest in their growth. It'll pay dividends in the long run.

Building a team isn't just about offloading tasks. It's about creating a machine that can grow beyond your personal limitations. It's about building something bigger than yourself.

The Bottom Line on Strategic Scaling

Okay, let's bring this home. Scaling isn't about working yourself into the ground or magically duplicating yourself (though wouldn't that be nice?). It's about creating a business that can grow beyond your personal limitations.

Remember these key points:

1. Systems are your secret weapon. They're what allow you to deliver consistent results without burning out.

2. Expansion is about leverage, not hustle. Use what you've already got and make it work harder for you.

3. You can't do it alone. Building a team isn't just helpful - it's essential for true scaling.

Now, I'm not going to give you some crazy to-do-list or challenge. Real scaling doesn't happen overnight. But here are three actions you can take right now to start your scaling journey:

1. Pick one process in your business and create an SOP for it. Make it so detailed that anyone could follow it.

2. Choose your best piece of content and repurpose it into two other formats. Blog to video, podcast to social posts - whatever works for you.

3. Identify one task you're currently doing that could be delegated. Write a job description for

someone to take this over.

These might seem like small steps, but they're the foundation of a scalable business. Remember, every empire starts with a single brick. You've got the blueprint - now it's time to start building.

Your future scaled, systematized, team-powered business is waiting. Go make it happen.

Chapter Eight

Overcoming Common Fears and Obstacles

From Paralysis to Powerhouse

Let me tell you about my client, Alex S.

Let me set the scene: It's a regular weekday afternoon, and Alex is sitting in front of his computer, his cursor hovering over the *"Go Live"* button on Facebook. His palms are sweaty, his heart's racing, and he's fighting the urge to slam his laptop shut and call it quits.

Alex had about 1,500 friends on Facebook at the time. Not a huge following, but not too shabby either. He knew going live could be a game-changer for his business, but man, was he terrified.

You want to know how long it took Alex to finally hit that *"Go Live"* button?

Three and a half hours.

Yeah, you read that right. For 210 agonizing minutes, Alex battled every fear and self-doubt in the book. What if he stumbled over his words? What if no one showed up? What if everyone thought he was a fraud?

But here's the thing - Alex did it. He faced his fears, pushed through the paralysis, and went live.

Was it perfect? Hell no. But it was a start.

And you know what happened next?

Alex kept showing up. Day after day, live after live. He pushed through the fear, learned from his mistakes, and gradually built his confidence.

Fast forward to today, and Alex's social media following has exploded to over 600,000. He's built the business of his dreams, impacting lives and crushing his goals.

All because he was willing to face his fears and take that first terrifying step.

Now, I'm not sharing this story to make you think that overcoming your fears is easy, or that success happens overnight. It doesn't.

What I want you to take away from Alex's journey is this: Your fears are normal. Your doubts are common. But they don't have to stop you.

In this chapter, we're going to dive deep into the fears and obstacles that hold so many coaches and entrepreneurs back.

More importantly, we're going to arm you with practical strategies to overcome these hurdles. Because here's the truth: every successful entrepreneur you admire has faced these same fears and obstacles. The difference is, they didn't let these challenges stop them.

And neither will you.

So, are you ready to turn your fears into fuel and your obstacles into opportunities? Let's dive in and start transforming those business-blocking fears into stepping stones for success.

———————— • ————————

Overcoming Obstacles

As you likely already know... Building a coaching business isn't all sunshine and rainbows. If you've been at this for more than five minutes, you've probably faced more obstacles than a contestant on American Ninja Warrior. But here's the thing - it's not about avoiding obstacles. It's about learning to hurdle over them like a boss (or ninja)

In this chapter, we're diving into the nitty-gritty of the mental and market challenges that can trip you up. We're talking fear, imposter syndrome, overwhelm, market saturation - all those fun little gremlins that like to pop up and whisper "you can't do this" in your ear. Spoiler alert: they're wrong, and I'm about to show you why.

Addressing Fear of Failure, Imposter Syndrome & Overwhelm

Let's start with the unholy trinity of entrepreneurial mind-f*cks: fear of failure, imposter syndrome, and overwhelm. If you haven't experienced at least one of these, are you even really in business?

Fear of Failure: News flash: failure isn't fatal. In fact, it's a crucial part of success. Every *"failure"* is just data - information about what doesn't work, pushing you closer to what does. So next time you're paralyzed by fear of failure, try this:

1. *Ask yourself:* "What's the worst that could happen?" Then ask, *"Could I handle that?"* Spoiler: you probably can.

2. *Reframe "failure" as* "experiment." You're not failing, you're collecting data.

3. Set micro-goals. Big goals are great, but they can be overwhelming. Break them down into smaller, less scary chunks.

Imposter Syndrome: Ah, good old imposter syndrome. That delightful feeling that you're a fraud and someone's going to find out any minute. Here's the truth: if you're worried about being an imposter, you're probably not one. Real imposters don't worry about this stuff. Try these tactics:

1. Keep a *"wins"* folder. Every time you get a compliment, a testimonial, or achieve something, stick it in there. Review when imposter syndrome

hits.

2. Remember: you don't need to know everything. You just need to know more than your clients and be a few steps ahead.

3. *Embrace the* "yet." You're not an imposter; you're just not where you want to be... yet.

Overwhelm: Feeling like you're drowning in to-do lists? Join the club. But overwhelm doesn't have to be your default state. Here's how to tackle it:

1. Brain dump everything. Get it all out of your head and onto paper.

2. Prioritize ruthlessly. What actually needs to be done now? What can wait? What can be delegated or deleted?

3. Focus on one thing at a time. Multitasking is a myth. Pick one task, do it well, then move on.

Strategies for Dealing with Market Saturation

"But Jason, the market is so saturated!" I hear this all the time, and guess what? It's bull*hit. Yes, there are a lot of coaches out there. But there's only one you. Here's how to stand out in a *"saturated"* market:

1. **Niche Down:** Don't be a general life coach. Be the go-to coach for introverted entrepreneurs who want to build a personal brand without feeling sleazy. The more specific, the better.

2. **Own Your Unique Story:** Your experiences, your journey, your perspective - that's your secret sauce. Don't be afraid to let it shine in your marketing.

3. **Focus on Results, Not Services:** Nobody cares about your 12-week program. They care about the transformation it provides. Sell the outcome, not the process.

4. **Create a Signature System:** Package your expertise into a unique, branded system. It makes you stand out and positions you as the expert (like

you did in Chapter 2... right?!)

5. **Be Where Others Aren't:** If everyone's on Instagram, maybe it's time to dominate LinkedIn. Zag when others zig.

Remember, market saturation is often just an excuse. There's always room for quality, authenticity, and real results.

Maintaining Confidence and Motivation

Let's be honest - some days, you're going to want to throw in the towel and apply for a job at Starbucks. (Hey, at least there's free coffee, right?) But before you dust off that resume, try these strategies for keeping your confidence and motivation high:

1. **Celebrate Small Wins:** Did you post content consistently this week? Book a discovery call? Even send that email you've been procrastinating on? Celebrate it. Every step forward counts.

2. **Surround Yourself with Positivity:** Join mastermind groups, connect with other coaches, unfollow negative nellies on social media. Your environment shapes your mindset.

3. **Revisit Your Why:** Remember why you started this journey. Write it down, create a vision board, whatever works. Just keep it front and center.

4. **Invest in Personal Development:** The more you grow, the more confident you'll become. Read books, attend workshops, hire your own coach. Never stop learning.

5. **Practice Self-Care:** You can't pour from an empty cup. Make time for exercise, meditation, hobbies - whatever fills you up.

6. **Set Realistic Expectations:** Rome wasn't built in a day, and neither is a successful coaching business. Be patient with yourself and celebrate progress, not perfection.

The Bottom Line on Overcoming Obstacles

Here's the deal - obstacles are part of the journey. They're not roadblocks; they're growth opportunities in disguise. Every time you overcome one, you're leveling up not just your business, but yourself.

So the next time fear creeps in, or you're feeling like an imposter, or the market seems too crowded, remember

this: you've got what it takes. You wouldn't have this dream
if you didn't have the capacity to achieve it.

Chapter Nine

Community Cultivation

Your Marketing Ally

Can Community Spirit Truly Bind Us?

Let me take you back to where it all began - my outdoor fitness center in South Florida.

We turned an abandoned roller-hockey rink (with a sink hole in it) - into a turfed out, fully equipped fitness center. Ohhh yeah and a whole lot of Florida sunshine (and humidity, let's be real).

When I first started, I thought my job was just about creating killer workouts and helping people get fit. Boy, was I wrong.

See, what I didn't realize at first was that I wasn't just building a fitness center. I was creating a community.

It started small. A few regulars would show up day after day, rain or shine. They'd chat before class, encourage each other during workouts, and hang around after to swap healthy recipes or share their progress.

As the weeks went by, something magical started happening. These people weren't just coming for the workouts anymore. They were coming for each other.

I remember one day, a new member joined us. She was shy, clearly uncomfortable, and looked like she was ready to bolt at any second. But before I could even make my way over to welcome her, three of my regulars had already surrounded her, introducing themselves and assuring her she was going to love it.

That's when it hit me: I wasn't just a fitness coach. I was a community builder.

So I leaned into it. I started organizing group challenges, hosting weekend hikes, and even set up a bulletin board where members could share their wins and struggles.

The results? Mind-blowing.

My little outdoor gym exploded. We went from a handful of regulars to over 200 members. And the best part? I barely had to market at all. Word of mouth did all the heavy lifting for me.

People weren't just signing up for a gym. They were joining a tribe.

Fast forward to today, and that lesson has become the cornerstone of my online coaching business.

When I first transitioned online, I'll admit, I was a bit lost. How could I recreate that sense of community in a virtual space?

But then I remembered - community isn't about a physical location. It's about connection.

So I got to work. I created a private Facebook group for my clients. I hosted weekly live Q&A sessions. I encouraged members to share their wins, no matter how small.

And you know what? That same magic from my outdoor fitness center started happening online.

Clients began cheering each other on. They shared recipes, swapped tips, and supported each other through tough times. Just like in the park, they weren't just there for my coaching - they were there for each other.

The impact on my business has been huge. My retention rates skyrocketed. Referrals started pouring in. And my marketing? It became so much easier because I had an army of raving fans doing it for me.

In this chapter, we're going to dive deep into how you can cultivate this kind of community in your own business. Whether you're running a physical location or an online coaching program, the principles are the same.

Remember, in a world where people are craving connection more than ever, building a strong community isn't just good for your business - it's good for your soul.

———————————— • ————————————

Harnessing the Power of Community in Coaching

Let me tell you something...
If you're not building a strong community around your coaching business, you're leaving *a lot* on the table.

In 2024 (and beyond), building a community isn't just a "nice-to-have." It's your secret weapon. It's how you create loyalty, drive organic growth, and build a coaching brand that *lasts*.

Think of it like this: **You're not just gathering an audience—you're building a tribe**. A community that believes in what you do, trusts you, and becomes your biggest advocates. That's not just a buzzword. It's the difference between coaches who grind endlessly for new clients and those who have clients coming to them—on repeat.

So let's break this down.

Building Your Online Tribe

Here's the first truth: **A community isn't just a bunch of people in a Facebook group.** It's a *living, breathing network* of people who are aligned with your brand, your values, and the transformations you offer.

When done right, your community becomes a **support system** where people share their struggles, their wins, and their stories. It's a place where your clients feel seen, heard, and connected—not just to you, but to each other. That connection? **It's the glue that makes them stay loyal** to your coaching practice.

And let me tell you—loyal clients are the ones who turn into your best advocates. They're the ones who talk about you, who refer their friends, and who stick around for the long haul.

Engagement: The Heartbeat of Retention

You want clients to stick around? Then you need to keep them engaged. Period.

Here's the deal: **Engagement is everything.** It's the heartbeat of your community, and without it, you've got nothing. If your community feels like a ghost town, people are going to check out faster than you can say "next client, please."

The more active and engaged your community is, the more valued your clients feel. And guess what? **Valued clients stick around.** They see the community as part of their journey, not just some side benefit. They're more likely to invest in your services again and again.

So how do you keep engagement alive? Simple. **You create a space where conversations never die.** Regular Q&As,

interactive polls, member shout outs—this is how you keep your community buzzing. When you create that kind of vibe, your clients aren't just customers—they're invested in the bigger picture.

Word-of-Mouth: The Organic Growth Engine

Let me hit you with a reality check: **Word-of-mouth is the most powerful marketing tool you have.** It's organic, it's authentic, and it doesn't cost a dime.

If your community loves what you're doing, they're going to tell people about it. They're going to share their wins, their experiences, and their breakthroughs. And when they do? **Your reach explodes.** Suddenly, you've got new clients knocking on your door without spending a single dollar on ads or promotion.

Here's how you make it happen: **Deliver so much value that your clients can't help but talk about you.** Whether it's through exclusive content, amazing coaching sessions, or just a supportive environment, you need to give them something worth talking about.

And if you really want to crank up the heat? **Put a referral system in place.** Give your community members incentives to bring in new clients. It's like rolling a snowball downhill—the more it rolls, the bigger it gets. Before you know it, your community is growing, and your business is thriving.

The Big Picture

When you bring these three things together—building a tribe, keeping them engaged, and leveraging word-of-mouth—you're not just growing your coaching business. You're creating a movement.

Your clients aren't just clients anymore. They're advocates, ambassadors, and walking proof of what you can deliver. That's what makes a community powerful. It's what keeps your clients coming back and brings new ones to your doorstep without you having to chase them down.

And here's the kicker: This all happens organically. No hard selling. No chasing leads. Just genuine connection, real engagement, and people talking about you because they want to.

If you're ready to turn your coaching business into a powerhouse that runs on community-driven growth, this is how you do it.

It's not just about getting more clients. It's about building something bigger—a community that propels your business forward while giving your clients the support they need to thrive.

Let's dive into exactly how you make that happen.

Discover Methods to Build and Nurture an Online Community

Let's get tactical now.

Building an online community is like planting a garden. You need the right seeds (members), the right soil (platform), and regular care (engagement). Get this right, and your community will *thrive*—supporting your coaching business and driving organic growth.

Step one? Choose your platform. Facebook group, Skool, Circle, etc —whatever fits your audience's needs. But don't stop there. The platform is just the ground; the real magic happens when you start nurturing.

Step two? Plant the right seeds—**content that resonates**. Understand what your audience needs, what keeps them up at night, and deliver that through consistent posts, live interactions, and personal responses. This isn't about generic tips or basic advice. It's about creating content that speaks to their *specific struggles* and desires.

Imagine your community as a beehive. Everyone's buzzing about their transformations, sharing their wins, and helping each other out. The buzz builds more buzz. And when people see this energy? They want to be part of it.

The key here is **consistency**. Weekly Q&As, interactive polls, discussion threads, challenges—anything that keeps the energy high and the conversation alive. **Engagement fuels growth**, and when your community is vibrant, people stick around and new clients come naturally.

Chapter Ten

The Final Act

Bringing It All Together

Will She Find Her Unique Voice in a Sea of Sameness?

Let me tell you about my client, Sarah.

When Sarah first came to me, she was drowning in a sea of sameness. She was a health coach, one of thousands out there, all saying pretty much the same thing.

"Eat clean, exercise more, drink water."

Sound familiar?

Sarah was posting content religiously, following all the *"rules"* of online marketing. But despite her efforts, her business was flatlining. Some engagement but inconsistent leads and sales.

I remember our first call like it was yesterday. Sarah's voice was heavy with frustration as she said, *"Jason, I'm doing everything right. Why isn't it working?"*

As we dug deeper, the problem became clear. Sarah's message was lost in the noise. She was saying what she thought she should say, not what she truly believed. She was trying to be everything to everyone, and in the process, she'd lost herself.

"Sarah," I asked, *"what makes you angry about the health industry?"*

There was a long pause. Then, like a dam breaking, Sarah let loose.

She ranted about the diet culture, the shame tactics, the unrealistic standards. She shared her own struggles with disordered eating and how she'd found healing through self-compassion and intuitive eating.

As she spoke, her voice changed. The frustration was replaced with passion. Her eyes lit up. This was the real Sarah, and she was magnetic.

"That," I said, pointing at her through the screen, *"That's your voice."*

Over the next few months, we worked on infusing Sarah's true voice into her content. We ditched the generic "clean eating" advice and instead focused on her message of healing your relationship with food.

It wasn't easy. Sarah was terrified of alienating people, of being "too much." But slowly, she found the courage to speak her truth.

And then, something magical happened.

Her content started to resonate. Comments flooded in from women who felt seen for the first time. Shares and saves skyrocketed.

But the real breakthrough came when Sarah got this message:

"Your post about ditching food guilt saved my life. I've started therapy because of you. Thank you for being real."

Sarah called me in tears that day. *"Jason,"* she said, *"I finally feel like I'm making a difference."*

From that point on, there was no stopping her. Sarah's business exploded. She went from struggling to fill a small group program to launching a course with over 500 students.

All because she found the courage to use her unique voice.

Remember, in a world where everyone's trying to fit in, the real power lies in standing out. Your unique voice isn't just your most powerful marketing tool - it's your legacy.

———— • ————

Stand Out or Stand Aside: Mastering the Art of Differentiation in a Saturated Market

The coaching world is crowded—packed to the brim with voices clamoring for attention. But here's the thing: the ones who stand out aren't just loud; they're *different*. This chapter isn't about tying things up with a neat little bow—it's about giving you the tools to not just survive in a saturated market but to thrive in it.

You've made it this far, and you've learned how to build a business from the ground up. But now comes the real test. In a world full of noise, how do you ensure your voice rises above the rest?

The key? *Mastering differentiation.*

Saturation Isn't Your Enemy — It's Your Opportunity

You've heard it before—*"the market is saturated."* And that's enough to make any coach cringe. But here's a little-known secret: saturation means there's a demand. And when there's demand, there's opportunity. Your job? Make sure you're the coach people *need*, not just another option.

Forget trying to be everything to everyone. That's a surefire way to blend in. Instead, get crystal clear on what makes you different and why that matters to your audience. You don't just want to be different—you want to be *indispensable*.

You've Got the Tools — Now Put Them to Work

Everything you've learned in this book has been building to this. From crafting your messaging to attracting the right clients, it all comes together in this chapter. This is where you take those insights and turn them into a strategy that solidifies your place in the market.

Let's recap:

- **Crafting your message:** You've learned that your message needs to cut through the noise. No fluff, no filler. Just a clear, compelling message that hits home with your audience.

- **Client attraction:** It's not about casting a wide net; it's about being a magnet for the right people. You're not chasing clients anymore—they're coming to you.

- **Conversion mastery:** Once you've grabbed their attention, you know how to convert that interest into action. You've got the formula, now apply it.

Final Words of Encouragement

You've come a long way, but remember, success isn't a one-time event—it's a habit. The market is competitive, no doubt, but it's also full of potential. The coaches who rise to the top aren't necessarily the ones with the most experience—they're the ones who adapt, who innovate, and who take action.

Now, it's time for you to take the next step. This chapter isn't just a recap—it's a launchpad. A launchpad that will send your business to the next level. From refining your messaging to scaling your operations, the steps are laid out for you.

Your edge in a saturated market? *Relevance.* If you're not speaking directly to the needs of your audience, you're getting lost in the shuffle. So focus on delivering value that resonates deeply and consistently.

Recap of Key Points

Let's take it from the top:

- **Clarifying Your Message:** Think of this as your beacon. The clearer your message, the stronger your connection with your audience. Don't just communicate—captivate.

- **Crafting a Powerful Narrative:** It's not about sharing facts; it's about telling a story that resonates. You want people to feel like they're part of the journey, not just observers. Your story is what makes you stand out from the rest.

- **Creating Strategic Content:** Content isn't just about being seen; it's about being remembered. Make sure your content speaks directly to your ideal client, answers their questions, and positions you as the authority.

- **Conversion Campaigns:** Getting attention is one thing—converting it into action is another. You've learned that campaigns should not only drive traffic but lead to meaningful engagement and sales.

- **Lead Nurture Systems:** Once you've captured leads, you need to nurture them through the buying journey. Implement systems like your Connection Block and Strategic Content Distribution System to build trust and relationships over time.

- **Building a Cash Conversion Machine:** Effective lead nurture leads to conversion. It's not enough to simply gather leads; you need systems in place (like workshops and live trainings) that convert these leads into paying clients, consistently driving revenue.

Recap: From messaging clarity to crafting compelling narratives, and creating content to running conversion campaigns, each step elevates your business, making it both impactful and profitable.

Words of Encouragement

You're standing at the edge of something big. But here's the thing—no one else can walk this path for you. You've got the map. You've got the tools. Now, it's time to *move*.

Success isn't about grand gestures—it's about persistence. The kind of persistence that shows up every day, even when it's tough. Just like a river carves through rock over time, your consistent effort will carve your path to success.

In moments of doubt, remember why you started. Your passion for helping others is the compass that will keep you on course. Let that passion fuel you when the going gets tough, and let it remind you that the impact you're making is real.

Final Recap and Encouragement

Throughout this journey, we've explored what it takes to go from a struggling coach to a six-figure business owner. And you've learned the strategies that will get you there. From attracting the right clients to converting leads into cash, every chapter has been a stepping stone.

And now, it's time to walk the path.

The market may be saturated, but that's not your problem anymore. You've got the tools, the strategy, and the mindset to stand out. So go out there and show the world why you're the coach they've been waiting for.

Stay focused, stay driven, and let your passion and purpose be the guiding light. Success isn't just possible—it's inevitable if you stay the course.

Chapter Eleven

Why You Might Need A Mentor

Mentoring, in its modern format, has been around since the late 1990s. People still think of it as something new, but in reality, mentoring has been around for millennia. There has never been a period in the history of humanity where mentors did not exist.

Sure, it might have looked a little different, but mentoring is as old as the hills. Modern day mentoring may be more refined and a lot more commercially viable, but the principles remain the same.

What Does a Mentor Do?

Mentors have the skills and knowledge to advise, support, and encourage their clients.

They help them to:

- Make sound decisions

- Take effective actions

- Resolve their challenges in the most efficient way possible

- Learn from the process, so they can repeat it whenever they want

- A mentor also has the ability to remain detached from the issues at hand.

Consider the wise words of Albert Einstein:

"We cannot solve our problems with the same thinking we used when we created them."

Time Is Money

In the modern era, in life and business, time is money. There's an ever-increasing amount of cooperation and collaboration going on both in businesses and in people's private lives. We need to figure things out almost on the fly these days while dealing with different time zones and cultures.

Everyone has their own unique issues to handle alongside everything else that needs to be accommodated, and then there's the technology we all use to connect with everybody and everything.

Life is definitely more complex today, and it certainly seems to speed up every time you turn around. It doesn't take long before we begin to have thoughts of overwhelm and burnout on our minds.

The question we need to ask ourselves is this: *"How long can I justify spending time and money on this issue trying to figure it out for myself, knowing what Albert Einstein said about problem solving?"*

If having a mentor could save you time and money, it would be ridiculous NOT to hire one, wouldn't it?

Throughout history, every King has had an Advisor (Mentor) in every culture. Every military leader has had a Strategist (Mentor), every World Class Athlete has had a trainer (Mentor), and every Entertainer has had a Manager (Mentor).

Who Hires a Mentor?

The only conclusion we can draw from the history of mentoring is that the people who hire a mentor fall into two camps:

- People who are at the top of their game and want to stay there, or

- People who aspire to be at the top of their game and want to get there as fast as they can

Many people will say that they want to change themselves, their life, their job, or their circumstances, but in real terms, they are fearful of change. They delay, procrastinate, and make excuses. They lack self-confidence and the drive to follow through. It's human nature. It's what ordinary people always do.

People who hire a Mentor are not ordinary people.

They are inspired and have vision. They embrace change and are prepared to get fully engaged in making positive changes in their life. Plus, they don't want it to take forever!

They have a sense of urgency, and they want someone they can lean on, confide in, use as a sounding board, and rely on to help them make the inevitable tough decisions that they can see on the horizon.

People hiring their first mentor are often racked with pessimism. They think, *"What if I waste my money?"*

Consider that, before you hire a mentor, you're already wasting time, which is the same as money, and you lack the resources to resolve the issues at hand. It would cost you less to hire a mentor and find out first-hand and NOW how unbelievably useful a mentor can be.

People who are hiring their second or subsequent mentor have no pessimism. What they are looking for is the perfect fit for them and the circumstances they find themselves in.

Within reason, money is not the issue and they never think about the possibility of wasting it.

Their primary concern is finding the RIGHT mentor and then hoping that the mentor they choose has a spot left open where they can be accommodated, and can they start today?

Is Hiring a Mentor Right For You?

Maybe. Maybe not.

- Are you at a point where NOT taking action is costing you time and money?

- Do you feel stuck in your struggles?

- Could you use encouragement and sage advice in moving forward?

If you answered "yes" to any of these questions, perhaps a mentor can get you moving in the right direction to help you create the life you desire - and sooner rather than later. If hiring a mentor seems right for you, or you're not sure if hiring a mentor is the best path for you, feel free to schedule a free call with me at https://tinyurl.com/be-in-demand. I'll help you determine if it's the right decision for you. No risk, no obligation. Just me helping you determine your best course of action.

Chapter Twelve

What you should do now...

Here's How To Get Started On That Healthy And Fit Business You Have Always Dreamed Of...

WE'VE REACHED THE END of our time together, my friend. I sincerely hope that you've benefited from reading my book in more ways than one.

The next step for you is simple:

Get started!

Now, it's time to take action. Nothing changes until you make the first move, and now you've got the tools and insights to transform your business.

Still unsure where to start or how to implement everything?

That's exactly what I'm here for. If you're ready to take the next step and want my help to build that profitable, in-demand coaching business, let's connect. I help coaches just like you create real momentum, scale to $20k-$30k months, and make a bigger impact—all without the stress or overwhelm.

Here's how we'll make it happen together:

1. **Step 1:** We'll start by dialing in your messaging, goals, and strategies to ensure we're building your business around what's truly aligned with you.

2. **Step 2:** We'll implement these strategies into your current routine so they fit seamlessly into your busy life.

3. **Step 3:** We'll fine-tune everything to create a system that consistently brings in clients, revenue, and results, without burning you out.

4. **Step 4:** Once everything is in motion, I'll help you track your progress and make any adjustments needed to maximize results as

quickly as possible.

Most coaches think they're stuck where they are—struggling to get clients, burning out on content, and feeling like that next level is out of reach. The truth? It's not. My done-with-you program is designed to make growing your business easy, stress-free, and sustainable.

If you're ready to build a business that brings you both impact and income—while keeping your sanity—let's talk. Schedule a free with me call at https://tinyurl.com/be-in-demand, and we'll take the next step together.

Epilogue

Crafting Your Future: A Guide to Consistent Success

We've covered a lot of ground in this guide, but this is where the real journey begins. You didn't just read through strategies and tactics to let them sit on a shelf. Now's the time to *apply* them, to take what you've learned and put it into action, shaping your business into the thriving enterprise you've envisioned.

The principles in these pages aren't just theory—they're tested, battle-proven steps in the competitive world of online coaching. If you use them, you'll go from playing small to dominating your market.

Recap of Key Strategies: Here's the bottom line: we've walked through how to know your market better than they know themselves, how to craft messaging that feels like it's reading their minds, and how to turn attention into paying clients that stick around for the long haul.

These strategies are more than just business tips—they're your *edge* in a crowded market. They're what's going to make you the go-to coach when your competition is still blending into the background.

Guidance for Implementation: Start by assessing what you're doing right now. Is your marketing clear? Are your client interactions building trust and setting you up as the authority? If not, tweak it. Every message, every touchpoint needs to scream *high value*.

Consistency is key here—because when you're consistent, your clients start to believe in your brand as much as you do.

But here's the thing—no strategy is foolproof forever. Markets change. Client expectations evolve. That's why the true secret to long-term success is staying sharp, continuing to learn, and being willing to adapt as you gather more data on what works and what doesn't. This book? Consider it your launchpad. Use it as the foundation, but build on it as you grow.

Take Action Now: The worst thing you can do after reading this is nothing. *Decisive action* is what separates those who succeed from those who just dream about it. Take what you've learned, refine your marketing, understand your market, and improve your systems.

Every step you take gets you closer to that stable, thriving business you've been working toward. This is how you create momentum, how you make growth inevitable.

A Lasting Impression: This isn't a book to read once and forget. It's your playbook for navigating new challenges, for revisiting when you need a fresh perspective or feel stuck. Success doesn't happen in one leap—it's a series of consistent, focused steps.

Remember this quote:

"Success is not final; failure is not fatal: It is the courage to continue that counts." –
Winston Churchill

Let that sink in. Success is never a straight line. It's full of ups and downs. What matters is that you keep going, refining, and growing through every challenge.

About the Author

Who is Jason Meland?

Jason Meland is more than just a coach—he's a visionary who helps fitness professionals turn their passion into thriving online businesses. With a relentless commitment to personal growth and an unmatched expertise in  messaging, content, and marketing strategy, Jason has built a reputation for transforming unheard coaches into in-demand brands.

Starting his journey as a gym owner and fitness coach himself, Jason understands the grind of building a business from the ground up. But after spending years stuck in the cycle of posting content, chasing leads, and feeling like he was constantly playing catch-up, he realized there had to be a better way. That's when he began mastering the art of storytelling and messaging—a discovery that shifted everything.

Today, Jason runs a 7-figure business helping other coaches break free from the hustle and find their voice in a crowded market. His proven systems help fitness entrepreneurs attract quality leads, convert them into high-ticket clients, and scale their businesses to consistent $20k-$30k months—all without the burnout of aggressive sales tactics.

Jason's work is rooted in authenticity, impact, and sustainable success. He believes every coach has a unique story and message that can make them a magnetic force in their industry. Through his coaching programs, workshops, and mentorship, Jason has helped countless coaches find freedom—both financially and personally—by building businesses that align with their values and goals.

When he's not coaching or writing, Jason enjoys time with his wife, Amanda, and their two kids, Ava and Jackson, making the most of his family life while pursuing his mission to change lives.

In his book, Jason offers a blueprint for creating an impactful coaching business while staying true to who you are. Because, at the end of the day, your business should be as extraordinary as you are.

Business name: In Demand Coach

Email: jason@indemandcoach.com

Website: www.indemandcoach.com

Made in the USA
Las Vegas, NV
14 November 2024